Romantic
Staffordshire Ceramics

Jeffrey B. Snyder

Schiffer Publishing Ltd

4880 Lower Valley Rd. Atglen, PA 19310 USA

To Sherry, with love.

Acknowledgments

I wish to express my gratitude to all of the people who made this book possible. Dealers and collectors allowed me into their shops and homes, permitting me to disrupt their lives and clutter their homes and work places with my tangle of equipment. Others were very generous with their knowledge (sharing photographs of their collections which unfortuantely could not be included in this text) and their encouragement. I offer my thanks to each of these individuals: James & Elizabeth Dunn, Bittersweet Antiques; L.B. Gaignault; Martha Jelinski; Dora Landey, South Salem, New York 10509; M. R. Markowitz; Par Esq., Los Angeles, California; John Potter, Keeper of Records, Friends of Blue, England; and Lisa Worden, Sloane Square Antiques. These people were instrumental in making this book possible.

Copyright © 1997 by Schiffer Publishing, Ltd.
Library of Congress Catalog Card Number: 97-80045

Designed by Bonnie M. Hensley

ISBN: 0-7643-0336-8
Printed in Hong Kong
1 2 3 4

Published by Schiffer Publishing Ltd.
4880 Lower Valley Road
Atglen, PA 19310
Phone: (610) 593-1777; Fax: (610) 593-2002
E-mail: Schifferbk@aol.com
Please write for a free catalog.
This book may be purchased from the publisher.
Please include $3.95 for shipping.

Please try your bookstore first.
We are interested in hearing from authors
with book ideas on related subjects.

Table of Contents

Introduction

Andalusia platter by William Adams & Sons, c. 1830. 15.5" x 13". *Courtesy of James & Elizabeth Dunn, Bittersweet Antiques.* $375-415.

An attractive unidentified floral pattern decorates this handleless cup and saucer, manufacturer unknown, c. 1830-40. Cup: 2.75" high x 3.5" wide; saucer: 5.5" in diameter. *Courtesy of James & Elizabeth Dunn, Bittersweet Antiques.* $70-75 cup and saucer set.

Below: **Napier** teapot by John and George Alcock, c. 1839-46. Part of a three piece set complete with a teapot and covered sugar bowl. 6.75" high x 10.5" wide. *Courtesy of James & Elizabeth Dunn, Bittersweet Antiques.* $925-1025 for the three piece set.

The term Romantic Staffordshire, as used in this book, covers a broad range of transfer printed patterns produced in England's Staffordshire potting district from roughly 1820 to the 1860s. The Staffordshire potting district was a major center of British ceramics manufacturing. By the middle of the nineteenth century a total of 133 factories, fully two-thirds of England's potting industry, would call Staffordshire home. The district encompassed the towns of Burslem, Cobridge, Dresden, Etruria, Fenton, Longport, Longton, Hanley, Shelton, Stoke-on-Trent, and Tunstall. Stoke-on-Trent provided Staffordshire with a rail hub.(Jewitt 1877) The patterns produced by Staffordshire's potters that are referred to today as "romantic" include scenic and city views of England and exotic foreign lands (some of which bear a striking resemblance to the location identified while others are pure romantic fiction), domestic scenes, sporting scenes, and a large number of patterns overflowing with fruit, flowers, shells, and/or birds.

This book provides a survey of some of the many thousands of Romantic Staffordshire transfer printed designs produced in England during the nineteenth century. Most of the patterns presented here were given names by their potters. However, the collector will soon find that there are distressingly large numbers of patterns that were never identified in any way by their manufacturers.

The Evolution of Transfer Printed Patterns From 1815 to 1860

The details of the transfer printing technique — an early and very successful form of mass production developed in England during the eighteenth century and perfected in the nineteenth — will be discussed later. However, to provide a better grasp of the scope of patterns included under our heading Romantic Staffordshire, a brief review of the evolution of transfer printed patterns from 1815 to 1860 is provided here.

The period from 1815 to 1835 saw transfer prints rise to their greatest heights of creativity and quality. With England free from the Napoleonic Wars and the War of 1812, opportunities for trade were opening up with huge markets in North America, Europe, India, and the east. Even the British home market was expanding. Virtually every potter in England was busy producing transfer printed earthenware ceramics as rapidly as possible for sale at home and abroad. This rise in demand for English dinner ware, combined with many potters' desire to place a different transfer printed pattern on every shape in a service, had designers of transfer prints

scrambling for new and unusual patterns. Coysh and Henrywood state that Enoch Wood & Sons alone used over fifty different patterns for a single dinner service. These are grouped in series of patterns to maintain some sense of organization. (Coysh & Henrywood 1982 (1), 10)

Providing inspiration for the harried pattern designers and engravers of this period was a Hampshire clergyman, William Gilpin. Mr. Gilpin toured England around the turn of the nineteenth century, writing and illustrating scenery books as he went. His theories on scenery and his aquatint scenes stirred the imagination of many, producing a subsequent flood of illustrated travel books. In England, the resultant fervor for scenic views became known as the "cult of the picturesque." As a mark of true success, Gilpin's efforts were satirized, first in verse by William Coombe between 1809 and 1811 and then in three volumes of aquatints by Thomas Rowlandson entitled *Doctor Syntax in Search of the Picturesque.* These were reproduced as transfer printed patterns on dinner ware which sold well in the American market. (Coysh & Henrywood 1982 (1), 10)

Designers snatched up the illustrations in the travel books and quickly applied these scenic views to the ever growing dinner ware stock. Series of patterns from

Below and right: **A View in Venice** dinner plate by William Ridgway, Italian series, c. 1830-34. 10.25" in diameter. *Courtesy of James & Elizabeth Dunn, Bittersweet Antiques.* $85-90.

this period, produced predominantly in cobalt blue, bear such names as "Antique Scenery", "British Views", "Italian Scenery", and "Picturesque Scenery". Many of the views produced were based on the works of some of England and Ireland's finest artists. The patterns produced were usually surrounded by a border pattern. Border patterns were often floral designs, many of which also feature small designs inside decorative medallions. The same border was used for a complete dinner service. Many potters used specific border designs as their signature trade mark. However, both the central patterns and the border designs were blatantly copied by other pottery manufacturers during this period. (Coysh & Henrywood 1982 (1), 10)

The Staffordshire transfer printed dinner services of this period were aimed at the growing Victorian middle class. This middle class was on the rise, taking advantage of the many economic opportunities presented by the Industrial Revolution. Dinner wares with finely crafted transfer prints were both impressive and inexpensive enough to attract buyers from this upwardly mobile social class.

Pheasant platter by Ridgway & Morley, c. 1840s. 13.25" x 11". *Courtesy of James & Elizabeth Dunn, Bittersweet Antiques.* $275-305.

The decade from 1835 to 1845 saw an improvement in transfer printing techniques but a decline in the quality of the images transferred onto dinner wares. The popular cobalt blue color, the mainstay of transfer printing until this time, was set aside from time to time for green, mulberry, and sepia colors. At times, the patterns from this period were also produced in two colors.

The decline in quality was a direct result of the durability and quality of the ceramics produced from 1815 to 1835. The growing Victorian middle class had been attracted by the quality of the wares and saw no reason to buy additional patterns from 1835 to 1845 because their original dinner, tea, and chamber sets had not broken. Middle class purchases of transfer printed wares dropped off. As a result, potters and engravers were forced to seek consumers with less financial clout. To provide affordable wares to farmers and factory workers, transfer printed patterns were standardized and the wares they were applied to were more cheaply manufactured. (Coysh & Henrywood 1982 (1), 10)

British Lakes covered vegetable dish by Stevenson, c. 1832-35. 11.5" long x 10.5" wide. *Courtesy of James & Elizabeth Dunn, Bittersweet Antiques.* $300-330.

For our purposes, the last period of interest encompasses the years from 1845 to 1860. The patterns produced during these years were radically affected by the English Copyright Act of 1842. This law allowed for the registration of original designs, design which once registered could not be copied for three years. Registered designs could also be renewed. Gone were the days when a designer could pick up a book and copy the images of famous artists. To fill the void, designers began producing imaginary romantic scenes which were decidedly formulaic. The proscribed romantic scene usually included a centrally located body of water, either a lake or a river. To one side would stand some edifice of classical architecture, the nationality of which was up to the engraver to determine while considering his target market. On the other side of the water a large tree should grow in the foreground. Beneath the tree an urn, a fountain, or a pillared balcony should rest. Mountains in the background and people in the foreground were preferred. A family dog or an artful grouping of barn yard animals was sometimes helpful. Some of these scenes bear the titles of actual towns and rivers; however, the image and reality rarely matched. Despite the lack of imagination of most of these romantic patterns, the quality of some of the transfer printed earthenwares remained high. (Coysh & Henrywood 1982 (1), 10-11; Snyder 1995, 36)

The Romantic Staffordshire transfer print decorated wares in this book were produced during these three periods and reflect the changing qualities and appearances of the prints throughout these decades. A few of the decidedly Eastern patterns, however, harken back to an earlier period when "chinoiserie" patterns were all the rage. All of the patterns presented here were printed on a strong white earthenware most commonly referred to as ironstone.

The English Earthenware Body — In Search of the Perfect White

Earthenwares are ceramic wares with soft, water-absorbent bodies made impermeable by glazing. Glazes, consisting of lead sulfides with additives introduced to add color or opacity to an otherwise colorless and transparent substance, were applied over these bodies, rendering them non-porous and resistant to chippage.

The ironstone earthenwares decorated with Romantic Staffordshire transfers were, in part, an end-product of English potters' quest for an inexpensive earthenware body which could compete with the Chinese export porcelains that had been taking Western markets by storm since the seventeenth century. (Tippett 1996, 7; Pratt 1982, 104-105) Between the last quarter of the eighteenth and the first quarter of the nineteenth century, British potters would achieve this goal, developing several earthenware bodies presenting a surface white enough to rival the coveted Chinese porcelains. The English wares were also durable enough to survive difficult trans-oceanic voyages to foreign markets.

Creamware and Pearlware

Creamware and pearlware were the English potters' early attempts to find that elusive white yet inexpensive earthenware body that would wrest the ceramics market out of the hands of Chinese potters and exporters. During the second half of the eighteenth century, English potters, particularly those of the Staffordshire district, refined their earthenwares. The bodies became thinner and harder. The body color was lightened to nearly that of the coveted Chinese porcelain's white. After 1750 these improvements led to creamware, a thin, hard-fired, cream colored earthenware dipped in a clear glaze. Josiah Wedgwood may have perfected creamware, or "Queen's Ware," in 1762. From 1765 to the early 1770s Josiah Wedgwood then experimented with the potting of a ware whiter than creamware which he christened "Pearl White" (pearlware) in 1779. By increasing the flint content in the body of the ware itself and adding a small quantity of cobalt to the glaze to offset the bodys natural yellow tint, Wedgwood presented a ware with a very white surface.

By 1787 there were at least eight factories known to have been producing pearlware under the guise of "china glaze, blue painted" in Burslem alone. One of the factories also proclaimed itself an "enameller and printer of cream colour and china glaze ware."

By the early 1800s, pearlware would so completely eclipse creamware as to reduce the latter to the cheapest tableware on the market. Pearlware came to be used for everything from dining services to chamber pots; however, it appeared most frequently in the form of shell-edged plates with rims painted either blue or green.

Creamware plate decorated with a black transfer printed peacock pattern, manufacturer unknown, c. 1790-1810. 7.5" in diameter. *Courtesy of James & Elizabeth Dunn, Bittersweet Antiques.* $145-160.

Whitewares, Semi-Porcelains and Ironstones

In the 1820s, pearlware would be replaced by earthenwares christened with a wide variety of descriptive names emphasizing either their brilliant whiteness or their immense strength. These names included whitewares, semi-porcelains, Spode's "Stone China," and Mason's "Ironstone China." (Snyder 1992) Charles James Mason's famous "Ironstone China," patented in the Staffordshire Potteries in July of 1813, was considered the best of these new earthenware bodies. The name alone conveyed a sense of strength associated in the public mind with Chinese ceramics. It was not long before most potters from 1830 through 1880 were producing their own version of ironstone under any number of inventive names. Some of the creative names applied to ironstone include "Granite China," "Opaque China," and "Stone China."

At their best, ironstone wares closely rivaled porcelain. However, for everyday use they had the upper hand. Ironstone ceramics were used for everything from table and tea services to toilet wares and foot baths during the nineteenth century. For Romantic Staffordshire they were the enduring wares of choice. Romantic Staffordshire designs were applied to ironstone earthenware ceramics.

British Dominance of the Nineteenth Century Ceramics Market

Industrialization provided British potters with the means to create and disseminate the most rapidly growing stock of durable, white earthenware bodies in human history; transfer printing allowed them to quickly produce large numbers of identically decorated wares from this stock for the first time in potting history. Together these new, white earthenware bodies and the transfer printed patterns would provide a popular, quality ware at a fairly low price, a ware many families of modest means could afford.

This combination of a durable, quality ware and well crafted, mass produced decoration helped propel Britain into dominance of the international ceramics marketplace. The popular Romantic Staffordshire patterns were quickly spread over the globe anywhere the British Empire could reach.

About the Values in the Captions

Values vary immensely according to the condition of the piece, the location of the market, and the overall quality of the design and manufacture. Condition is always of paramount importance in assigning a value. Prices in the Midwest differ from those in the West or East, and those at specialty antique shows will vary from those at general shows. Of course, being in the right place at the right time can make all the difference.

All of these factors make it impossible to create an absolutely accurate price list; however, a useful general pricing guide can be offered. The values reflect what one might realistically expect to pay at retail or auction and are listed in U.S. dollars.

Napoleon supper plate by Charles James Mason and Company, c. 1829-44. 9.25" in diameter. *Courtesy of James & Elizabeth Dunn, Bittersweet Antiques.* $85-90.

Chapter 1.
Origins and Development of Transfer Printing

Transfer printing allowed a potter to quickly duplicate a pattern by transferring it from a copper plate to a ceramic vessel via a specially treated paper. Transfer printing appealed to the pottery manufacturers as it was much quicker and cheaper than the hand painting techniques used prior to its introduction. Transfer printed patterns appealed to consumers as the process afforded them the opportunity to purchase complete sets of dishes that were virtually identical, a feat never before possible with the hand painted wares.

John Brooks, an Irish engraver, is credited with the first successful use of the transfer printing technique. He applied for a patent for printing on enamels and china on September 10, 1751. In 1753, John Brooks was registered as a partner in the firm Janssen, Delamain & Brooks, at an enamel factory at York House, Battersea, London. While the firm of Janssen, Delamain & Brooks probably produced the earliest transfer prints in red and purple on white salt-glazed plates, John Sadler and Guy Green of Liverpool are recognized for perfecting the technique in 1756. On July 27, 1756, Sadler and Green reported that they were able to print "upwards of twelve hundred earthenware tiles of different patterns ..." in six hours. Sadler and Green produced black prints on delftware (a very soft bodied ware) and creamware. The early transfer prints were applied over top of the glaze. The "overglazed" patterns quickly showed signs of wear when used and were only truly suitable for decorative pieces which were never subjected to hard use. Printing in underglaze blue on earthenwares would not become common until the end of the eighteenth century. (Noël Hume 1969, 128-129; Little 1969, 13-14)

Underglaze printing was first used about 1760 on English porcelain, which was over twenty years before its introduction on Staffordshire earthenwares. Underglaze cobalt blue printing on earthenwares was introduced around 1783 in Staffordshire. Cobalt blue was discovered to be the only color early on that would survive the high firing temperatures necessary for underglazing the design.

Once transfer printing was accepted by potters as a decorative technique, it quickly gained popularity with the public. The earliest patterns were deep cobalt blue Chinese designs. The earliest transfer printed "chinoiseries" were printed on pearlware.

Around 1802, wide (predominantly floral) borders became popular. Various potteries developed characteristic border designs which were rarely copied. Print quality improved during the early nineteenth century as engravers learned to use dots instead of lines to create their patterns through stippling. The dots acted as a shading device which provided greater perspective to the prints. The earliest dated ware with stippled engraving is from 1807.

The overall quality of the art work varied according to the resources of both the potter and his customers. The leading firms produced beautiful ceramics with finely engraved transfer printed patterns. Lesser firms produced simpler designs, frequently following the lead of their larger competitors.

Around 1810, prints of English and foreign landscapes began to appear frequently on Staffordshire wares as well. These patterns, although remaining popular until approximately 1860, began to be replaced in the 1830s by strictly romantic views.

Production of Transfer Prints

Transfer printing became a respected and powerful mass production tool. It enabled a pottery to reproduce many copies of the same pattern quickly with the aid of predominantly semi-skilled laborers, and without the expense of employing many trained artists. However, an engraver with an artist's touch was essential to producing beautiful transfer printed patterns. Large pottery manufacturers had their own engravers while the smaller companies purchased patterns from engraving firms.

Romantic Staffordshire ceramics were decorated with underglaze transfer printed designs so that the patterns were sealed and could not wear off with frequent use. To create a successful design, the engraver first sketched his pattern and adapted it to fit every ceramic piece in the service. When he was satisfied with the design, the engraver transferred the patterns for the various wares to copper plates. Once transfered, the pattern lines were engraved. When the engraving was complete, burrs raised along the edges of the etched lines were scraped smooth and any areas of the pattern requiring darker shades of color or deeper shadows were etched again. (Copeland 1980, 21)

Trial prints of the new pattern were then pulled onto ceramic bodies to guarantee that, once fired, the final image would be all it was expected to be. If the pattern proved to be correct, the etched copper was plated with nickel, and later steel, to extend the pattern's working life. The nickel or steel plating decreased the chances that the copper plate's surface could be scratched, adding unwanted extra lines to the pattern. (Copeland 1980, 22)

When the pattern was approved, it was up to transferrers to correctly place the central images and border pieces of the print. These women carefully matched joins and arranged prints around spouts, finials, and handles. The match lines, however, are often visible. Even more interesting is what happens to transfer printed wares containing inscriptions. Hastily engraved copper plates provided transfers that had to be cut and trimmed to fit vessels of different sizes instead of providing a separate sized transfer for each vessel. The trimming and fitting process often led to nearly illegible inscriptions as letters were cropped off here and there. Pictures often remained whole but words suffered, not that it mattered to the women fitting the pattern; few of them could read. For that matter, many of the customers could not read either.

Once the specially treated transfer paper holding the inky pattern was successfully applied, the back of the paper was gently rubbed with a small piece of felt to transfer the design. The paper was then rubbed down with a stiff-bristled brush to ensure that the color had been completely transferred to the porous earthenware biscuit.

Once transferred, the paper was washed away and the biscuit bearing its new design was glazed, placed in a protective fire saggar, and fired in the kiln. Transfer printed designs were used only when a relatively long run of a particular design was required. No one went to the expense of engraving a copper plate for a single object or even a small run and no one ever engraved a costly set of coppers for a service, if only a few were to be made. With these restrictions it is easy to see that no printed design was ever unique. There were no one-of-a-kind issues in transfer printing.

The first successful color used in underglazed transfer printing during the eighteenth century was deep cobalt blue. Cobalt blue was the only color which could withstand the high temperatures used during early underglazing and was the mainstay of underglazed transfer printing by 1776.

In 1828 new underglaze techniques allowed black, green, yellow, and red enamels to be transferred. This resulted in prints with two or more colors. The process was expensive, however, with each color requiring its own transfer and a separate firing. The early deep cobalt blue color was replaced with new synthetic blues around 1845. In 1848, multiple color underglazing techniques were further advanced in England, allowing three colors (red, yellow, and blue) to be applied in a single transfer with only one firing. Green and brown were added in 1852.

The manufacturer's mark, often incorporating the name given to the transfer printed pattern, was engraved on the same copper plate as the main design. These were laid down at the same time as the main pattern. The manufacturer's mark usually provided the pattern name, the initials or name of the maker, and in many cases the town where the factory was located. Once transferred to the paper the mark was cut off and applied to the backs of plates or to the bases of hollow wares. Marks were omitted at times for a variety of reasons.

While these marks are one of the best and easiest clues in identifying a piece, a few of them will always remain a mystery. There were so many manufacturers, producing such enormous quantities of wares, that not all the marks were identified. Also, some potters stayed in business for such a short time and made so few pieces that the identity of their marks have been lost to history. Additionally, many small firms saw no reason to use marks as these tiny manufacturers had no name recognition value.

Palestine dinner soup plate and luncheon plates in blue, black, pink, plum, green, brown, and red by William Adams. 10.5" diameter dinner plates; 8" diameter luncheon plates. *Courtesy of L.B. Gaignault.* Dinner soup plate: $120-130; luncheon plates: $75-80; side plate: $60-65.

Chapter 2.
Manufacturers' Marks and Registration Marks

Dating Romantic Staffordshire with Manufacturers' Marks and Components of the Marks

Romantic Staffordshire ceramics often, but not always, carry manufacturers' marks on the undersides of flatwares (plates, platters, etc.) or along the bottoms of hollowwares (pitchers, tureens, etc.) and are frequently accompanied by the name given to the central pattern or pattern series. Manufacturers' marks first-and-foremost identify the potter by name and frequently include both the potter's symbol and the city location of the firm. For a firm with a long history, these marks are particularly helpful in dating the wares on which they are found. The marks were periodically changed and, when the marks of each period are well recorded, ceramics bearing a specific mark can be dated to a specific period of production.

Manufacturers' marks on Romantic Staffordshire are usually found in one of two forms: impressed marks, which were pressed into the unfired earthenware body's underside or base with a tool reminiscent of a branding iron, and transfer printed marks applied above or beneath the glaze.

Specific features were added to manufacturers' marks at particular dates. The guidelines which follow provide dates of introduction for key elements of British manufacturers' marks.

1800 — All printed marks occur after 1800

1810 — Marks incorporating the name of the pattern postdate 1810

1810 — The English Royal Coat of Arms appear on marks after 1810

1830 — "Published by," a term in use from c. 1830 to 1840 referring to the English 1797 Sculpture Copyright Act.

1838 — Victorian quarter arms appear in 1838

1840 — Round or oval shaped garter-like marks appear in 1840

1842 — Diamond-shaped registration marks are applied along with manufacturers' marks in 1842 in compliance with the Copyright Act of that year and cease to be used after 1883

1850 — "Royal" becomes a common term attached to many manufacturers' trade names after 1850

1860 — "Limited" or its abbreviation (Ltd.) is incorporated into English manufacturers' marks in 1860 and beyond after an English act of law establishes them in 1855

1863 — "Trade Mark" applied to English wares from 1863 onward in accordance with the Trademark Act of 1862

Registration Marks and Registration Numbers

Romantic Staffordshire wares post-dating 1842 include those pesky English registration marks associated with the Copyright Act of 1842 which led to the development of so many "romantic" patterns. Beginning in 1842, English decorative art designs were registered at the British patent office, seriously limiting the range of subjects available for reproduction on Romantic Staffordshire wares. However, not every registered piece was marked.

A diamond-shaped registry mark was used between 1842 and 1883. The layout of the information within the diamond was altered after 1867. The registration mark in use from 1868 to 1883 and the subsequent registry number introduced in 1884 are beyond the scope of this book.

The diamond-shaped registry marks in use from

This is an example of the registration mark in use from 1842 to 1867. Reading the codes, the date of registry recorded here is February 17, 1852. *Courtesy of L.B. Gaignault.*

1842-1867 contained a series of letters and numbers in specific locations around the diamond that had the following meanings:

1) the large Rd was the abbreviation for "registered";
2) the Roman numeral in the circle above the apex of the diamond mark represented the type of material used in the production of the marked ware;
3) the letter within the semi-circle below the apex of the diamond represented the year of registry;
4) the Arabic numeral to the right of the Rd abbreviation represented the day of the month of registry;

5) the Arabic numeral below the Rd abbreviation represented the parcel number, which was a code indicating the person or company who registered the pattern or the ware;
6) the letter to the left of the Rd abbreviation represented the month of registry.

The following tables translate the registration code numbers and letters on the diamond-shaped registry marks.

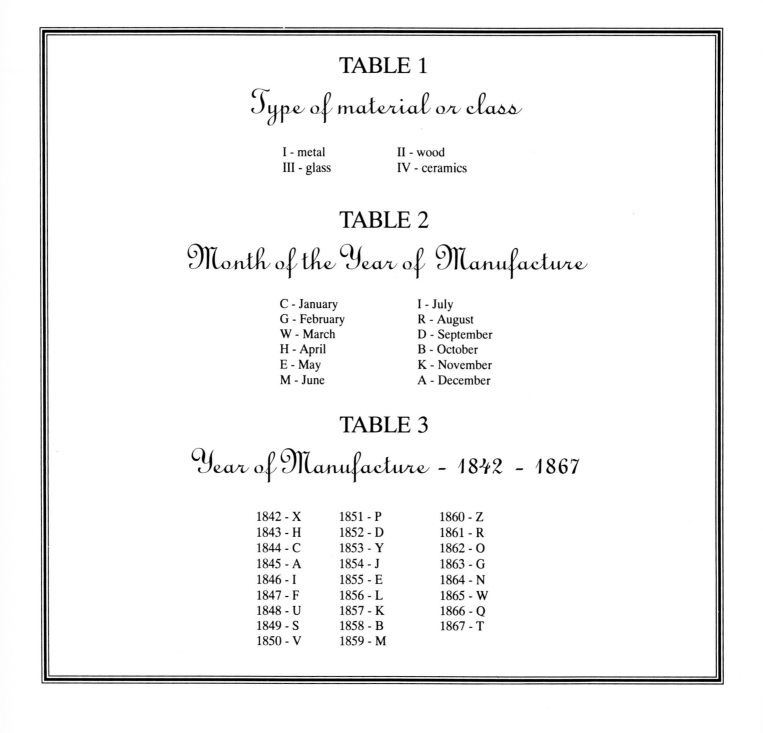

TABLE 1

Type of material or class

| I - metal | II - wood |
| III - glass | IV - ceramics |

TABLE 2

Month of the Year of Manufacture

C - January	I - July
G - February	R - August
W - March	D - September
H - April	B - October
E - May	K - November
M - June	A - December

TABLE 3

Year of Manufacture - 1842 - 1867

1842 - X	1851 - P	1860 - Z
1843 - H	1852 - D	1861 - R
1844 - C	1853 - Y	1862 - O
1845 - A	1854 - J	1863 - G
1846 - I	1855 - E	1864 - N
1847 - F	1856 - L	1865 - W
1848 - U	1857 - K	1866 - Q
1849 - S	1858 - B	1867 - T
1850 - V	1859 - M	

Chapter 3.
Manufacturers and Their Wares

The following is a survey of the Staffordshire potters and their Romantic Staffordshire wares. This is a solid sample of the patterns, their varying motifs, and the manufacturers (both large and small) that produced them. A brief description is provided for series of patterns, providing the names of the various scenes in the series whenever possible. If the displayed view is a single pattern that is not part of a series, no such description is provided.

References used throughout this section to provide detailed information about the potters and their romantic patterns and series of patterns included: *The Dictionary of Blue and White Printed Pottery 1780-1880* by A.W. Coysh and R.K. Henrywood (2 volumes); *Encyclopaedia of British Pottery and Porcelain Marks* by Geoffrey A. Godden; *Staffordshire Romantic Transfer Patterns* by Petra Williams (2 volumes); and *Historical Staffordshire* by Jeffrey B. Snyder.

The Adams Family

The Adams family produced many creative Staffordshire potters, all of whom appear to have had an unfortunate lack of creativity when it came to naming their sons. The Adams assert that 1657 is the date they established themselves as potters. The Adams family continues to produce ceramic wares today. During the first half of the nineteenth century, three cousins — all named William Adams — owned and managed several Staffordshire potteries. The William Adams born in 1745, once apprenticed to Josiah Wedgwood, operated out of Greengates, Tunstall from 1779-1805. He produced a variety of earthenwares including blue jasper wares with white reliefs in the Wedgwood style. On his death in 1805, his son Benjamin Adams ran the Tunstall operation, turning out high quality blue transfer printed pearlware impressed B. ADAMS.

The second cousin, William Adams, operating the Greenfield Works of Stoke-on-Trent from 1804-1829, specialized in blue transfer printed earthenware. Adams produced quality earthenwares enjoyed both in the home market and abroad. His offerings featured patriotic scenes, historical personages and scenic views for export to the United States. The Stoke-on-Trent works may have been the first to employ a steam engine for the grinding of their flints. The ceramic wares produced at this factory were considered comparable in style and quality to Wedgwood's wares. The Stoke-on-Trent works would pass out of the Adams family's hands in 1863.

The third cousin, William Adams, and his sons William and Thomas — son and grandsons of William Adams of Stoke-on-Trent — produced pottery at the Greenfield Works of Tunstall, under the name William Adams and Sons and produced the Ro-

mantic Staffordshire wares presented here. The Greenfield Works were originally established in Stoke-on-Trent by William Adams' father, who ran the works under his own name until 1829. In 1834, the Greenfield Works William Adams opened new works at Tunstall, placing his son William at the helm. According to Llewellyn Jewitt, a ceramics historian writing in the late 1870s, the firm experienced a dissolution in 1853 and the works were continued by William Adams (the father of William and Thomas) until 1865, when he retired. In 1865 the firm passed to his sons, William and Thomas.

Series and Views

Andalusia

This series of views presents dogs or horses together with the typical romantic accessories or gazebos. It is usually printed in pink.

Andalusia dinner plate by William Adams and Son, c. 1830s. 10.5" in diameter. *Courtesy of James & Elizabeth Dunn, Bittersweet Antiques.* $95-105.

Beehive

This is a variation on the romantic scene presented by William Ridgway & Company. It features a large beehive in the foreground and a flower vase in the distance.

Beehive small sauce bowl by William Adams & Sons, c. 1810-25. 6" in diameter. *Courtesy of James & Elizabeth Dunn, Bittersweet Antiques.* $20-22.

Bologna

A series of romantic scenes featuring gondolas surrounded by a border of floral and scenic vignettes overlaid on a geometric ground.

Bologna open vegetable dish by William Adams & Sons, c. 1835. 9" x 7". *Courtesy of James & Elizabeth Dunn, Bittersweet Antiques.* $145-160.

Bologna side plate by William Adams & Sons. 7.25" in diameter. *Courtesy of L.B. Gaignault.* $40-45.

Caledonia

A series of Scottish views featuring hunters wearing kilts. The views are surrounded by a medallion border.

Caledonia dinner plate by William Adams, 1820-1840. 10.5" in diameter. *Courtesy of L.B. Gaignault.* $100-110.

Below and right: **Chess Players** wash basin and pitcher by William Adams and Son, c. 1840. Bowl: 13.5" in diameter x 4.5" high; pitcher: 11" high. *Courtesy of James & Elizabeth Dunn, Bittersweet Antiques.* $ 850-935 set.

Columbia

A series of romantic views featuring centrally placed Eastern architecture and several people in the foreground. These views are printed in light blue.

Below and left: **Columbia** tureens and waste bowl by William Adams & Sons. The tureen on the right is decorated with the **Columbia** pattern on the outside and the **Navarrino** pattern on the inside. Tureens: 9.5" in diameter; waste bowl: 6" in diameter. *Courtesy of L.B. Gaignault.* Columbia tureen: $100-110; waste bowl: $75-80; Navarrino tureen: $75-80.

Columbus

A series of fanciful scenes chronicling the adventures of Christopher Columbus in the New World. The border features floral sprigs and animals.

Columbus platter by William Adams and Sons. 17" x 13.5" *Courtesy of James & Elizabeth Dunn, Bittersweet Antiques.* $480-530.

Columbus supper plate by Adams, c. 1836. 9.5" in diameter. *Courtesy of James & Elizabeth Dunn, Bittersweet Antiques.* $100-110.

Above two photos: **Columbus** dresser box by Adams, c. 1835. 4" high x 4.5" wide. *Courtesy of James & Elizabeth Dunn, Bittersweet Antiques.* $265-290.

Columbus coffee pot by William Adams. 12.5" high. *Courtesy of James & Elizabeth Dunn, Bittersweet Antiques.* $550-605.

17

Below and left: **Columbus** dinner plate by William Adams & Sons. 10.5" in diameter. *Courtesy of L.B. Gaignault.* $110-120.

Cyrene

Cyrene cup and saucer by William Adams & Sons. *Courtesy of L.B. Gaignault.* $75-80.

Delphi

A series of romantic scenes with ruins and figures surrounded by a border of scrolls and flowers.

Below and left: **Delphi** dinner plate by William Adams & Sons, 1800-1864. 10.5" in diameter. *Courtesy of L.B. Gaignault.* $95-105.

Cupid

A series of dark blue patterns which carry no printed names to identify the views. Three images are known featuring this chubby winged infant. They are:

Cupid; Cupid and Roses; Cupid and Virgin.

The **Cupid** series pattern on this dinner plate by William Adams & Sons has the viewer seeing double with two apparent cupids pausing to smell the roses. 10" in diameter. *Courtesy of Dora Landey.*

"Father Matthew, the Great Advocate for Temperance"

A pattern printed in black featuring the standing figure of Father Matthew exhorting a kneeling crowd to abstain from drinking. Beehive medallions surround the center image.

"Father Mathew, the Great Advocate for Temperance" cup and saucer by Adams, dating from c. 1810. Cup: 4" in diameter; saucer: 6" in diameter. *Courtesy of L.B. Gaignault.* $95-105.

Florence

Florence open vegetable dish by William Adams & Son. 8.5" x 6". *Courtesy of L.B. Gaignault.* $75-80.

Forget-me-not

Forget-me-not cup and saucer by Adams. Cup: 4" in diameter; saucer: 6" in diameter. *Courtesy of L.B. Gaignault.* $75-80.

Fountain Scenery

A series of romantic views, all of which feature a central fountain. These are found printed in both pink and blue.

Fountain Scenery platter by William Adams & Sons. 15.5" x 12.5" *Courtesy of James & Elizabeth Dunn, Bittersweet Antiques.* $395-435.

Gazelle

Gazelle covered sugar bowl with a flower finial by William Adams, c. 1800-30. 6.75" high. *Courtesy of James & Elizabeth Dunn, Bittersweet Antiques.* $160-180.

Genoa

Above and left: **Genoa** supper plate by William Adams & Sons. 9.25" in diameter. *Courtesy of L.B. Gaignault.* $75-80.

Habana

A series of views registered on July 26, 1845. The most recognizable common feature throughout is the series of circular medallions containing the images of nobles alternating around the rim.

Habana soup plate by William Adams & Son. Registered on July 26, 1845. 9.25" in diameter. *Courtesy of M. R. Markowitz.* $75-80.

Isola Bella

A series of light blue printed scenes with individuals in the foreground and romantic architecture located on the left, replete with arches, towers, and stairs.

Isola Bella pedestaled cake plate and cup plate by William Adams & Sons. Cake plate: 12.5" x 3" high; cup plate: 4" in diameter. *Courtesy of L.B. Gaignault.* Cake plate: $150-165; cup plate: $50-55.

Isola Bella luncheon plate by William Adams & Sons. 8.5" in diameter. *Courtesy of L.B. Gaignault.* $50-55.

Lions Pattern platter by William Adams & Sons. 19" x 14". *Courtesy of Dora Landey.*

Lorraine

Lorraine side plate by William Adams & Sons. 7.5" in diameter. *Courtesy of L.B. Gaignault.* $35-40.

Navarrino

A romantic scene with a central river or lake, a gondola-style boat loaded with people crossing that body of water in the center distance, a large tree on the right-hand side of the scene, and a large fortified structure nestled into the mountainside on the left. This scene if printed in light blue. (*see* Columbia, the image on the right is Navarrino.)

Palestine

A series of romantic scenes full of gazebos, tents, busy figures, and distant minarets.

Palestine plate by William Adams & Company. *Courtesy of James & Elizabeth Dunn, Bittersweet Antiques.* NP.

Palestine supper plate by William Adams, c. 1850. 9.5" in diameter. $50-55.

Palestine supper plate by William Adams. The back of the plate features an impressed "ADAMS" manufacturer's mark and printed pattern name. 9.25" in diameter. *Courtesy of James & Elizabeth Dunn, Bittersweet Antiques.* NP (No Price).

A very rare multi-colored **Palestine** pattern covered sugar bowl by William Adams, c. 1840. 6.5" high by 8" wide. *Courtesy of James & Elizabeth Dunn, Bittersweet Antiques.* $350-370.

Palestine water pitcher by Adams, c. 1840-50. 9" high. *Courtesy of James & Elizabeth Dunn, Bittersweet Antiques.* NP.

Palestine coffee pot by Adams. 11" high. *Courtesy of James & Elizabeth Dunn, Bittersweet Antiques.* $500-550.

Persia teapot by William Adams & Sons. 6.5" high. *Courtesy of L.B. Gaignault.* $200-220.

Palestine dinner plate by William Adams & Sons and Damascus supper plate. 10.5" and 9" in diameter. *Courtesy of L.B. Gaignault.* Dinner plate: $120-130; supper plate: $65-70.

Ruins saucer by William Adams & Company. 6" in diameter. *Courtesy of L.B. Gaignault.* $30-35.

The Sea

A series of nautical views chronicling various aspects of life at sea.

The Pirates pattern platter from **The Sea** series by William Adams & Sons. 13.5" x 11". *Courtesy of James & Elizabeth Dunn, Bittersweet Antiques.* $355-390.

The Sea luncheon plate by William Adams & Sons. 8.5" in diameter. *Courtesy of James & Elizabeth Dunn, Bittersweet Antiques.* $80-85.

The Sea supper plate by William Adams & Sons. 9.5" in diameter. *Courtesy of James & Elizabeth Dunn, Bittersweet Antiques.* $90-100.

Seasons

A series of patterns showing a man in the various seasons of the year. The names "WINTER" and "FEBRUARY" have been seen associated with the central scene and border vignettes contain the seasonal names "SPRING", "SUMMER", "AUTUMN", and "WINTER".

Seasons supper plate by William Adams. 9.5" in diameter. *Courtesy of James & Elizabeth Dunn, Bittersweet Antiques.* $90-100.

Seasons teapot by William Adams, c. 1830-40. Note: the word Spring is found on the lid, the word Summer around the lip, the word Winter is found toward the bottom of the teapot. 8" high x 11.5" wide. *Courtesy of James & Elizabeth Dunn, Bittersweet Antiques.* $230-255.

Seasons dinner plate by William Adams, c. 1830. 11" in diameter. *Courtesy of James & Elizabeth Dunn, Bittersweet Antiques.* $95-105.

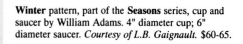
Winter pattern, part of the **Seasons** series, cup and saucer by William Adams. 4" diameter cup; 6" diameter saucer. *Courtesy of L.B. Gaignault.* $60-65.

Sower

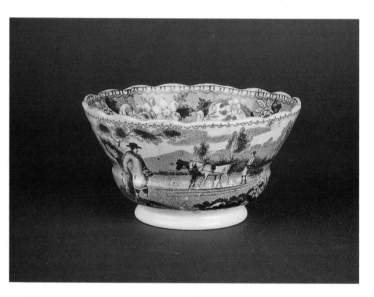

Sower covered sugar bowl by William Adams, c. 1800-30. 6" wide x 6" high. *Courtesy of James & Elizabeth Dunn, Bittersweet Antiques.* NP.

Center right and right: **Sower** waste bowl by William Adams, c. 1835. 3" high x 5.5" in diameter. *Courtesy of James & Elizabeth Dunn, Bittersweet Antiques.* $140-155.

Spanish Convent

A romantic series of religious scenes surrounded by a flower border.

Spanish Convent platter by William Adams, c. 1835. 17" x 13.5" *Courtesy of James & Elizabeth Dunn, Bittersweet Antiques.* $395-435.

An unidentified pattern featuring two bucks and three does adorn this platter by William Adams & Sons. 15.5" x 13". *Courtesy of Dora Landey.*

An unidentified pattern luncheon plate by William Adams & Sons. The back of the plate has a lightly impressed "ADAMS" manufacturer's mark in use on earthenware from 1800 to 1864. The pattern is similar to the unidentified pattern found on the side plate that was possibly produced by Davenport. 8" in diameter. *Courtesy of James & Elizabeth Dunn, Bittersweet Antiques.* $55-60.

Marks

The Adams family marks usually incorporate the family name, Adams. W. Adams & Sons used W.A. & S. or the firm's full name. A variety of impressed and printed backstamps were produced. Blue transfer printed wares destined for the United States were impressed with an eagle and also bore the printed name of the subject in a foliate cartouche. After 1829 W. ADAMS & SONS is the manufacturer's mark in use.

A rare multi-colored luncheon plate with an unidentified pattern by William Adams & Sons. 8" in diameter. *Courtesy of James & Elizabeth Dunn, Bittersweet Antiques.* $100-110.

William Adams & Sons (Potters) Ltd., Greengates and other locations, Tunstall and Stoke, impressed manufacturer's mark in use from 1804 to 1840. *Courtesy of Dora Landey.*

William Adams & Sons (Potters) Ltd., Greengates and other locations, Tunstall and Stoke, impressed manufacturer's mark in use from 1804 to 1840. *Courtesy of Dora Landey.*

The Alcocks

"...the finer descriptions of earthenware, one of their [Samuel Alcock's] specialities being semi-porcelain of fine and durable quality." — Llewellynn Jewitt, 1877.

Samuel Alcock produced pottery and porcelain in a wide variety of wares from Staffordshire from c. 1828-1859. Wares ranged from inexpensive domestic wares to finely crafted bone china and earthenwares. Alcock rebuilt an old Burslem pottery of Ralph Wood's in c. 1830, the Hill Pottery. While much of Samuel Alcock's work went unmarked, there were distinctive shapes employed which were registered and bear a registration mark. Each registered shape was produced in several sizes and decorated in a wide variety of designs. Samuel Alcock also employed a system of fractional pattern numbers. These help to identify his wares.

John Alcock produced earthenware ceramics in Cobridge from 1853 to 1861. After that date the firm was renamed Henry Alcock & Company (1861 to 1910). John Alcock produced the Cologne, Moselle, and Priory patterns in Romantic Staffordshire wares.

John and George Alcock were also established in Cobridge. They were producing earthenwares from 1839 to 1846. While Jewitt had nothing to say of their accomplishments, John and George Alcock produced Romantic Staffordshire in the Blantyre, Napier, Pompeii, and Vintage views. A partnership of John and Samuel Alcock, Junior succeeded John and George Alcock at Cobridge from c. 1848 to 1850.

Series and Views — John Alcock

Cologne

Cologne potato bowl by John Alcock. 10.75" in diameter. *Courtesy of L.B. Gaignault.* $120-130.

Moselle

Blantyre

Above and right: **Moselle** luncheon soup plate by John Alcock. *Courtesy of L.B. Gaignault.* $50-55.

Above and left: **Blantyre** side plate by John & George Alcock. 7.25" in diameter. *Courtesy of L.B. Gaignault.* $35-40.

Priory

Priory potato bowl by John Alcock (also produced by Henry Alcock). 11" in diameter. *Courtesy of L.B. Gaignault.* $150-165.

Napier dinner plate by John and George Alcock, c. 1839-46. 10" in diameter. *Courtesy of James & Elizabeth Dunn, Bittersweet Antiques.* $85-90.

Napier creamer by John and George Alcock, c. 1839-46. Part of a three piece set complete with a teapot and covered sugar bowl. 4.5" high by 6.5" wide. *Courtesy of James & Elizabeth Dunn, Bittersweet Antiques.* $925-1025 for the three piece set.

Napier covered sugar bowl by John and George Alcock, c. 1839-46. Part of a three piece set complete with a teapot and covered sugar bowl. 6.75" high x 8.5" wide. *Courtesy of James & Elizabeth Dunn, Bittersweet Antiques.* $925-1025 for the three piece set.

Napier child's teapot, creamer, and covered sugar bowl by John and George Alcock, c. 1840. Creamer: 3" high; teapot: 3" high; sugar bowl: 3" high. *Courtesy of James & Elizabeth Dunn, Bittersweet Antiques.* $265-290 set.

Napier teapot by John & George Alcock, c. 1830-46. 6.5" high x 10" wide x 5". *Courtesy of James & Elizabeth Dunn, Bittersweet Antiques.* $300-330.

Vintage

Vintage child's cup and saucer by John & George Alcock. 2.75" diameter cup; 4.5" diameter saucer. *Courtesy of L.B. Gaignault.* Child's cup and saucer: $60-65.

Vintage luncheon plate by John & George Alcock. 8.25" in diameter. *Courtesy of L.B. Gaignault.* $50-55.

Pompeii

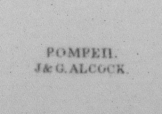

POMPEII.
J & G. ALCOCK.

Below and right: **Pompeii** dinner plate by John & George Alcock. 10.5" in diameter. *Courtesy of L.B. Gaignault.* $95-105.

Series and Views — Samuel Alcock & Company

Blenheim

Blenheim luncheon plate by Samuel Alcock. 8.25" in diameter. *Courtesy of L.B. Gaignault.* $50-55.

Commerce

A series of trading scenes, the example shown here is printed in light blue.

Commerce small sauce bowl by Samuel Alcock & Company, c. 1828. 6" in diameter. *Courtesy of James & Elizabeth Dunn, Bittersweet Antiques.* $34-37.

Maryland

Above and right: **Maryland** dinner plate by Samuel Alcock, 1830-1859. 10.25" in diameter. *Courtesy of L.B. Gaignault.* $75-80.

Left: **Commerce** supper plate by Samuel Alcock. 9" in diameter. *Courtesy of L.B. Gaignault.* $75-80.

Left: **Pearl** supper plate (part of a dinner set) by Samuel Alcock & Company, c. 1830-59. 9" in diameter. *Courtesy of James & Elizabeth Dunn, Bittersweet Antiques.* $60-65.

Below: **Pearl** platter (part of a dinner set) by Samuel Alcock & Company, c. 1830-59. 12.5" x 10". *Courtesy of James & Elizabeth Dunn, Bittersweet Antiques.* $150-165.

Samuel Alcock's marks were mainly printed. There were several including the name "S Alcock & Co." At times only the initials "S A & Co." were used.

Printed marks used John Alcock's full name and his "Cobridge" location.

John and George Alcock used impressed marks with the name "J & G ALCOCK" combined either with the "COBRIDGE" town name or with the name of the ceramic body "ORIENTAL STONE". Another ceramic body identification on their ironstone was "ALCOCKS INDIAN IRONSTONE". This firm also used the initials "J. & G. A." on several impressed or printed marks.

Sea Leaf dinner plate by Samuel Alcock. 10.5" in diameter. *Courtesy of James & Elizabeth Dunn, Bittersweet Antiques.* $95-105.

Printed "Pearl" pattern name and "Florentine China" name for the earthenware body manufactured by Samuel Alcock & Company, Cobridge, c. 1828-53, Hill Pottery, Burslem, c. 1830-59. *Courtesy of James & Elizabeth Dunn, Bittersweet Antiques.*

Samuel Alcock & Company, Cobridge, c. 1828-53, Hill Pottery, Burslem, c. 1830-59, impressed "ALCOCK" mark. *Courtesy of James & Elizabeth Dunn, Bittersweet Antiques.*

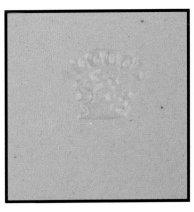

Statue

Statue sauce tureen by Samuel Alcock & Company. 6" high. *Courtesy of L.B. Gaignault.* $95-105.

Baker & Son

(W.) Baker & Company manufactured earthenwares at Fenton from 1839 to 1932.

Series and Views

Claremont

Above and left: **Claremont** supper plate and small open vegetable dish by Baker & Son. Supper plate: 9" in diameter; open vegetable dish: 7.25" wide. *Courtesy of L.B. Gaignault.* Supper plate: $75-80; open vegetable dish: $60-65.

Corrella

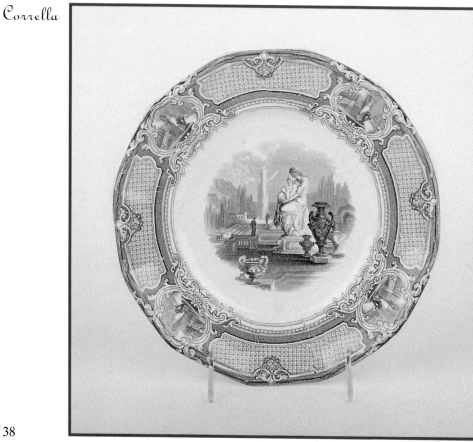

Left and above: **Corrella** luncheon plate by Baker & Son (later manufactured by Edge Malkin). 8.75" in diameter. *Courtesy of L.B. Gaignault.* $45-50.

Missouri

The romantic Missouri scene was registered on June 5, 1850.
(Coysh & Henrywood 1982, 249)

Above and left: **Missouri** wash basin and pitcher by Barker & Son. 13" diameter basin; 11" high pitcher. *Courtesy of L.B. Gaignault.* $500-550 set.

Marks

The names of individual patterns were often included in the manufacturer's marks from about 1860 onward. The word "Ltd." was added in 1893.

Barrow & Company

An example of a Doria pattern has been found marked "Barrow & Company."

Series and Views

Doria

Doria dinner plate by Barrow & Company. 10.25" in diameter. *Courtesy of L.B. Gaignault.* $65-70.

J. & M.P. Bell & Company

Earthenwares, Parian, and other ceramics were produced by J. & M.P. Bell & Company at Glasgow Pottery, Dobbies Loan, Glasgow, Scotland, from 1842 to 1928. The founders of this pottery were John Bell and Matthew Preston Bell. According to Coysh and Henrywood, their most impressive design was the "Triumphal Car." (Coysh and Henrywood 1982, 38)

Series and Views

Triumphal Car

Above and left: **Triumphal Car** covered butter dish and dinner plate by J. & M.P. Bell & Company. 9.5" diameter butter dish; 10" diameter plate. *Courtesy of L.B. Gaignault.* Covered butter dish: $150-165; dinner plate: 90-100.

Webster Vase

Webster Vase supper plate, possibly by J. & M.P. Bell. Note that this pattern has the same border as the **Domestic** pattern relish dish and cup and saucer also shown here. Plate: 9" diameter; relish dish: 9" long; cup: 3.75" in diameter; saucer: 5.75" in diameter. *Courtesy of L.B. Gaignault.* $60-65.

Marks

The initials "J. & M.P.B. & Co." were used as a manufacturer's mark from c. 1850 to 1870.

Booth & Meigh

The Rhine name was very popular during the Victorian period and was applied to patterns by Booth & Meigh, Thomas Fell & Company, J.T. Hudden, David Lockhart & Company, and the Middlesbrough Pottery Company.

Series and Views

Rhine

Rhine pitcher by Booth & Meigh. 8" high. *Courtesy of L.B. Gaignault.* $175-190.

William Bourne

William Bourne's firm produced prodigious amounts of blue and white printed wares from his Bell Works in Burslem from c. 1804 to 1818.

Series and Views

Lasso

This Lasso pattern is attributed to William Bourne.

Above and right: **Lasso** luncheon and side plates by William Bourne. Luncheon plate: 8.75" in diameter; side plate: 7.5" in diameter. *Courtesy of L.B. Gaignault.* Luncheon plate: $65-70; side plate: $50-55.

William & James Butterfield

William & James Butterfield produced earthenwares at the Globe Pottery, Tunstall, from 1854 to 1861. After 1861, the firm became W. & C. Butterfield.

Series and Views

Alma

Above and right: **Alma** supper plate by William & James Butterfield (Globe Pottery, Tunstall, 1854-61), "W. & J.B." printed manufacturer's mark. 9.25" in diameter. *Courtesy of L.B. Gaignault.* $45-50.

Marks

"W. & J.B." was used as the printed manufacturer's mark. Several individual printed marks were used in this period and pattern names were often included.

Edward Challinor

"The earthenware is of the ordinary common quality, specially designed and well adapted for the various markets to which it is sent." - Llewellynn Jewitt, 1877

Established at the Pinnock Works, Tunstall in 1842 continuing until 1867. Edward Challinor and E. Challinor and Company at the Fenton Potteries in Fenton from 1853-1867, followed by E. & C. Challinor at the Fenton Pottery in Fenton produced white granite, transfer printed, flown, and sponged for the export market. Tea, coffee, breakfast, and dinner services were produced along with toilet sets and other useful domestic articles.

Edward Challinor produced several Romantic Staffordshire series of patterns including Priory, Union, and an Oriental Sports series based on Spode's Indian Sporting Series. (Coysh and Henrywood 1989, 52)

Series and Views

Ardennes

Below and right: **Ardennes** supper plate by Edward Challinor. 9.75" in diameter. *Courtesy of L.B. Gaignault.* $75-80.

Corinthia

Corinthia pie plate and waste bowl by Edward Challinor. The pattern on the plate has five cartouches while the waste bowl has only four. Pie plate: 6.5" in diameter; waste bowl: 6" in diameter. *Courtesy of L.B. Gaignault.* Pie plate: $30-35; waste bowl: $60-65.

Lozère

Lozère cream jug and saucer by Edward Challinor. *Courtesy of L.B. Gaignault.* Cream jug: $75-80; saucer: $30-35.

Panama

Panama luncheon plate by Edward Challinor. 8" in diameter. *Courtesy of L.B. Gaignault.* $60-65.

Priory

Above and right: **Priory** dinner plate by Edward Challinor. 10" in diameter. *Courtesy of L.B. Gaignault.* $80-85.

Unidentified

An unidentified pattern supper plate by Edward Challinor. 9" in diameter. *Courtesy of James & Elizabeth Dunn, Bittersweet Antiques.* $85-90.

43

Union dinner soup plate by Edward Challinor. 10.5" in diameter. *Courtesy of L.B. Gaignault.* $110-120.

Marks

Edward Challinor used several printed marks with the company name or initials and with the pattern name often included. This pattern holds true for E. Challinor & Company (1853-1862) and E. & C. Challinor (1862-1891).

Joseph Clementson

Joseph Clementson became the sole proprietor of the Phoenix Works in Shelton, Hanley, in c. 1839 after a period of joint ownership as Reed & Clementson which began in 1832. Jewitt states that Clementson gained sole proprietorship shortly after the 1832 date. The works prospered and were expanded in 1845. In 1856 he purchased the Bell Works previously occupied by William Ridgway. Clementson's firm produced granite wares with white surfaces and with painted or printed decoration. The firm was known for high quality transfer printed designs. Much of Clementson's production was exported to America and Canada. Clementson produced a variety of Romantic Staffordshire patterns and series of patterns including Classical Antiquities, Palermo, and Sydenham. His sons succeeded him and traded as "Clementson Brothers" until 1916.

Classical Antiquities

The scenes in this series were registered on March 13, 1849 and include:

Homer Invoking the Muses; Juno's Command; Penelope Carrying the Bow to the Suitors; Ulysses at the Table of Circe; Ulysses Following the Car of Nausicaa; and Ulysses Weeps at the Song of Demodocus.

Classical Antiquities dinner and supper plates in a variety of colors and two scenes by J. Clementson. Dinner plate: 10.25" in diameter; supper plate: 9" in diameter. *Courtesy of L.B. Gaignault.* Dinner plate: $100-110; supper plate: $75-80.

Loretto

See Tessino.

Lucerne dinner plate by J. Clementson. 10.25" in diameter. *Courtesy of L.B. Gaignault.* $75-80.

Above and right: **Palermo** twelve-sided coffee can by Joseph Clementson. The importer's mark reads "Evans & Hill, Concord, NH, Importers." 3.5" in diameter. *Courtesy of L.B. Gaignault.* $150-165.

Siam

Siam open vegetable dish by Joseph Clementson. 9.5" x 12.5". *Courtesy of L.B. Gaignault.* $250-275.

Above and right: **Sydenham** green pie plate, waste bowl, and relish dish by J. Clementson. Printed on the back of the relish dish is the distributor's mark "Manufactured for Davenport Bros. 203 Greenwich St. N.Y." 6.25" diameter pie plate; 6.25" diameter waste bowl; 9" long relish dish. *Courtesy of L.B. Gaignault.* Pie plate: $25-30; waste bowl: $75-85; relish dish: $75-85.

Tessino

Above and right: **Tessino** (this is the same center scene as Loretto) supper plate and **Loretto** side plate by Joseph Clementson. 9.25" and 7.25" in diameter. *Courtesy of L.B. Gaignault.* Supper plate: $60-65; side plate: $35-40.

Right: **Basket and Vase Floral Pattern** coffee pot by James & Ralph Clews. 11.75" high x 9.5". *Courtesy of Dora Landey.*

Marks

Several printed marks bearing the name "J. CLEMENTSON" or the initials "J.C." are known. One mark used from 1840 onward has the Phoenix bird with the name "J. CLEMENTSON" underneath it.

James & Ralph Clews

James and Ralph Clews rented the Cobridge Works in Cobridge, Staffordshire from William Adams in 1815. The brothers specialized in high quality blue transfer printed wares during their partnership, which ended in 1834. They produced several pattern series including some for the export trade to America and Russia.

Clews produced several unique series. These were entitled the Doctor Syntax Series (based on William Combe's books printed from 1815-1821 lampooning the "cult of the picturesque"), the Wilkie's Designs Series (or Pictures of Sir David Wilkie), and the Zoological Series.

After the dissolution of the firm in 1834, James Clews sailed for America, joining the Indiana Pottery Company of Troy, Indiana, as one of three principals. He remained in the United States for five years.

Series and View

Basket and Vase Floral Pattern

Basket and Vase Floral Pattern (other side) coffee pot by James & Ralph Clews. 11.75" high x 9.5". *Courtesy of Dora Landey.*

Canovian supper plate by James & Ralph Clews, c. 1818-34. 9" in diameter. *Courtesy of James & Elizabeth Dunn, Bittersweet Antiques.* $70-75.

Bird of Paradise

Bird of Paradise wash basin by R. & J. Clews, c. 1830. 12.5" wide x 4.5" high. *Courtesy of James & Elizabeth Dunn, Bittersweet Antiques.* $345-370.

Genevese

Genevese dinner plate by James & Ralph Clews, c. 1818-34. 10.5" in diameter. *Courtesy of James & Elizabeth Dunn, Bittersweet Antiques.* $95-105.

"Hunting Dog" coffee pot by James & Ralph Clews. 9.25" high x 10.5". *Courtesy of Dora Landey.*

Unidentified

An unidentified pattern on an open vegetable dish by James & Ralph Clews, Cobridge Works, Cobridge, Staffordshire, 1815-1834, dating from c. 1820. 9.5" x 7.75". *Courtesy of James & Elizabeth Dunn, Bittersweet Antiques.* $145-160.

Impressed "CLEWS WARRENTED STAFFORDSHIRE" circular mark surrounding a crown. This mark was used from c. 1818 to 1834. *Courtesy of James & Elizabeth Dunn, Bittersweet Antiques.*

Unusual printed Clews manufacturer's mark reading "R. & J. Clews." *Courtesy of James & Elizabeth Dunn, Bittersweet Antiques.*

Clyde Pottery Company

The Clyde Pottery Company was operated by various managements at Greenock, Scotland, from its establishment in c. 1815 until its closure in 1903.

Series and Views

Gondola

Marked pieces from this pottery probably date from c. 1850 to 1903.

Robert Cochran & Company

Robert Cochran & Company produced earthenwares, stonewares, and china at the Verreville Pottery in Glasgow, Scotland, from 1846 to 1918.

Series and Views

Syria

Above and right: **Syria** dinner soup plate by Robert Cochran & Company. 10.25" in diameter. *Courtesy of L.B. Gaignault.* $70-75.

*Left:***Gondola** warmer plate, possibly by Clyde Pottery Company. *Courtesy of L.B. Gaignault.* $90-100.

This pottery used both the initials "R.C. & CO." and the name "R. Cochran & Co." on printed and impressed marks.

Cotton & Barlow

Cotton & Barlow potted their blue and white earthenware ceramics at Commerce Street, Longton, from 1850 to 1855.

Series and Views

Medina

Above and right: **Medina** supper plate by Cotton & Barlow. 9.75" in diameter. *Courtesy of L.B. Gaignault.* $50-55.

This pottery used the "C. & B." initials mark to identify its wares, frequently accompanied by pattern names.

Davenport

John Davenport bought and enlarged the Unicorn Bank works in 1794 in Longport, Staffordshire. Davenport began by producing cream-colored earthenware with well-painted and fine blue transfer printed designs. Later, stone china would be added to the earthenwares.

By c. 1805, Davenport was producing porcelain, which quickly led to the production of expensive fine porcelain lines. By 1810, Davenport was producing a wide range of domestic wares, vases, and a few figurines.

A dynamic export trade began in c. 1815. Ironstone bodies were produced in large quantities until the 1880s, destined for American shores. John Davenport's early transfer prints were considered to be high quality works. Some deterioration in quality occurred after 1830. Transfer printed wares would remain a staple of the firm throughout its life. Of Davenport's wares, Llewellyn Jewitt would remark, "Some of the cups ... are of elegant form, and those in blue and white, whether in pencilled, ordinary transfer printing or 'flown', are highly successful."

John Davenport retired a wealthy man in 1832. At that time his firm employed in excess of 1400 people. His sons carried the business forward until 1887. Beginning c. 1830 the firm was using a variety of ground colors, heavy gilding, and elaborate landscapes, well crafted flowers, and still life arrangements. In 1858, William Davenport took over the business. Davenport dessert services from the 1850s through the 1870s were highly regarded. The firm continued until 1881, when it became a private company, "Davenport & Company." The company finally closed in 1887.

Series and Views

Florentine Fountain

Chinese Pastime

Florentine Fountain luncheon plate by Davenport. 9" in diameter. *Courtesy of L.B. Gaignault.* $40-45.

Above and left: **Chinese Pastime** dinner plate by Davenport. 10.5" in diameter. *Courtesy of L.B. Gaignault.* $120-130.

Davenport

The Davenport pottery produced a series of scenes that were not titled and now referred to simply as "Davenport".

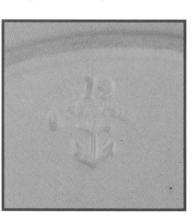

Far right and right: **Davenport** dinner plate by Davenport. The back of the plate has an impressed anchor and the name "DAVENPORT." 10.5" in diameter. *Courtesy of James & Elizabeth Dunn, Bittersweet Antiques.* $65-70.

Friburg

Friburg platter by William Davenport (also produced by G. Phillips). 13.5" x 10.5". *Courtesy of L.B. Gaignault.* $120-130.

Gondola

Gondola supper plate by William Davenport and Company. 9.5" in diameter. *Courtesy of James & Elizabeth Dunn, Bittersweet Antiques.* $85-90.

Montilla

Montilla nut dish by Davenport. 5.25". *Courtesy of L.B. Gaignault.* $30-35.

"Swiss Lake & Village"

"Swiss Lake & Village" gravy boat and dinner soup plate by Davenport. The impressed anchor mark indicates a date of 1836. 7.5" long gravy boat; 10.5" diameter plate. *Courtesy of L.B. Gaignault.* Gravy boat: $75-80; dinner soup plate: $100-110.

Unidentified

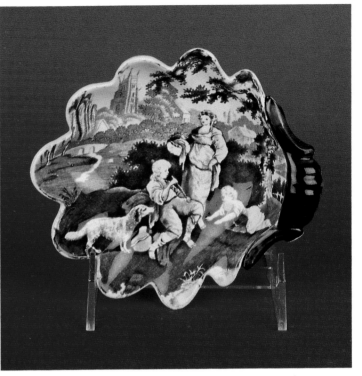

The Villagers nut dish by Davenport. 5.5" x 5". *Courtesy of Dora Landey.*

Unidentified pattern side plate by Davenport. The manufacturer's name "Davenport" is stamped on the back of the plate. 7" in diameter. *Courtesy of James & Elizabeth Dunn, Bittersweet Antiques.* $38-41.

The Villagers

This is the common name for the scene.

The Villagers foot bath by Davenport. 9" high x 15" wide x 18.5" long. *Courtesy of Dora Landey.*

The Villagers supper plate by Davenport. 9.75" in diameter. *Courtesy of Dora Landey.*

Marks

The earliest ceramics produced by John Davenport were unmarked. The first mark employed was a printed DAVENPORT in red with three small circles below. This was followed by the firm's name arced over an anchor. After 1806, DAVENPORT LONGPORT STAFFORDSHIRE printed on three lines might appear surmounted by the anchor. A crown appeared above the anchor after 1830 when a royal service was presented to William IV. By 1835, and possibly before, the impressed Davenport anchor is the distinguishing feature of the Davenport marks. Accompanying the anchor at times are the last two digits of the year placed on either side of the anchor. Davenport used a variety of printed and impressed marks including the name of the firm and often the pattern name. From 1850 onward the name DAVENPORT appeared in a semi-circular ribbon enclosing the now familiar anchor.[15]

Francis Dillon

Francis Dillon produced his earthenware pottery at Cobridge, from 1834 to 1843. Examples of his Romantic Staffordshire include Arabian, Asiatic View, and Gardening.

Series and Views

Arabian

Arabian handleless cup and saucer by Francis Dillon, c. 1834-43. Cup: 4" wide x 2.5" high; saucer: 6" in diameter. *Courtesy of James & Elizabeth Dunn, Bittersweet Antiques.* $65-70 cup and saucer set.

Asiatic View

Asiatic View luncheon plate by Francis Dillon, c. 1834-43. 8.5" in diameter. *Courtesy of James & Elizabeth Dunn, Bittersweet Antiques.* $55-60.

Gardening

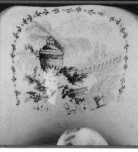

Above and right: **Gardening** creamer by Francis Dillon, c. 1834-43. Note the pattern on the lip. 5.5" high. *Courtesy of James & Elizabeth Dunn, Bittersweet Antiques.* $100-110.

Marks

Francis Dillon, Cobridge, printed "F.D." manufacturer's mark in use from 1834 to 1843. *Courtesy of James & Elizabeth Dunn, Bittersweet Antiques.*

Francis Dillon, Cobridge, printed "F.D." manufacturer's mark in use from c. 1834 to 1843. *Courtesy of James & Elizabeth Dunn, Bittersweet Antiques.*

Finely sculpted floral finial on the **Coral Border** covered vegetable dish. *Courtesy of James & Elizabeth Dunn, Bittersweet Antiques.* NP.

Thomas Dimmock

Thomas Dimmock (Junr) & Company produced earthenwares at Albion Street from c. 1828 to 1859, at Tontine Street from c. 1830 to 1850), and Shelton (also at Hanley) from c.1828 to 1859. Dimmock earthenwares were considered by the London jury of the first international exhibition of technology, commonly referred to as the Crystal Palace Exhibition, to be of first-rate quality. His patterns were admired for their neatness and good taste, for the general excellence of his wares.

Select Sketches

Rhodes is one of a series of sketches.

Left and below: **Rhodes Select Sketches** supper plate by Thomas Dimmock, 1828-1859. 9.25" in diameter. *Courtesy of M. R. Markowitz.* $60-65.

Series and Views

Coral Border

Left: **Coral Border** covered vegetable dish with a floral finial by Thomas Dimmock, c. 1828-59. The base measures 12.25" wide, 2.75" high; the lid measures 9" wide x 4" high. *Courtesy of James & Elizabeth Dunn, Bittersweet Antiques.* $360-395.

Marks

Thomas Dimmock used a less than definitive "D." printed initial manufacturer's mark. This mark appears in a number of different printed marks. Frequently the name of the individual pattern is also included. One note of caution, during the nineteenth century there were a number of potters named Dimmock working in Staffordshire.

Edge, Malkin & Company

This pottery operated out of Newport and Middleport Potteries in Burslem, from 1871 to 1903. It was previously known as Cork, Edge & Malkin, and after 1903 became S.W. Dean.

Series and Views

Goat

Italy cup and saucer by Edge, Malkin & Company. Cup: 3.5" in diameter; saucer: 5.75" in diameter. *Courtesy of L.B. Gaignault.* $45-50.

Marks

This company produced an impressed "EDGE, MALKIN & CO." mark and several printed initial marks.

James Edwards

James Edwards produced blue printed earthenwares at Dale Hall, Burslem from 1842 to 1882. James Rogers & Son had been the previous potter at Dale Hall. James Edwards brought his son Richard into the firm as a partner in 1851.

Series and Views

Corinth

Goat child's saucer by Edge Malkin & Company. 5" in diameter. *Courtesy of L.B. Gaignault.* $30-35.

Corinth supper plate and fourteen-paneled handled cup and saucer by James Edwards. Supper plate: 9" in diameter. *Courtesy of L.B. Gaignault.* Supper plate: $50-55; handled cup and saucer: $50-55.

Marks

The firm used both the full name and the initials "J.E. & S." in their marks, accompanied at times by "D.H." for Dale Hall.

James & Thomas Edwards

The partnership between James and Thomas Edwards was brief. Together they worked the Kilncroft Works and Sylvester Street in Burslem, Staffordshire from 1839 to 1841. Produced for the American market during this period was one registered design dating to 1841, "Boston Mails."

Series and Views

Mansion

This is a series of romantic scenes printed on dinner wares, all marked with the "Mansion" title.

Mansion dinner soup plate, possibly by James & Thomas Edwards. 10.25" in diameter. *Courtesy of L.B. Gaignault.* $120-130.

Sirius

Sirius platter by James and Thomas Edwards, c. 1839-41. 17" x 14.5" *Courtesy of James & Elizabeth Dunn, Bittersweet Antiques.* $450-495.

Marks

James and Thomas Edwards used several printed or impressed marks including "J. & T. E.", "J. & T. EDWARDS" with the letter "B" below the name for Burslem, or the simple "EDWARDS" mark.

Thomas Edwards

Thomas Edwards produced ceramics on his own briefly around 1841 in Burslem. Llewellynn Jewitt stated that Edwards owned the Swan Bank Pottery and Waterloo Pottery. (Coysh & Henrywood 1982, 125)

Series and Views

Hudson

Above and right: **Hudson** dinner plate by Thomas Edwards, 1839-1841. 10" in diameter. *Courtesy of L.B. Gaignault.* $90-100.

Waverley

Above and right: **Waverley** dinner plate by Thomas Edwards, c. 1841. 10" in diameter. *Courtesy of L.B. Gaignault.* $75-85.

Marks

Thomas Edwards is known to have used an impressed "T. EDWARDS" mark.

Temple

Left and above: **Temple** platter by Thomas Edwards. 13.5" x 10.5". *Courtesy of L.B. Gaignault.* $175-190.

Elkin, Knight & Bridgwood

This pottery produced china and earthenwares at The Foley Potteries of Fenton from c. 1827 to 1840. The company had previously been known as Elkin Knight & Company and Elkin Knight and Elkin.

Series and Views

Etruscan

A series featuring patterns with classical figures.

Above and right: **Etruscan** soup plate by Elkin, Knight & Bridgwood. 10.5" in diameter. *Courtesy of L.B. Gaignault.* $130-140.

Marks

This pottery used printed initial marks "E.K.B." and were often accompanied by the pattern name.

Thomas Fell & Company

Thomas Fell produced creamwares, earthenwares, and other ceramics at St. Peter's Pottery, Newcastle upon Tyne, Northumberland from 1817 to 1890. The addition of "& Co." was added to the name around 1830.

Series and Views

Antiquarian

Antiquarian supper plate, possibly by Thomas Fell & Company, c. 1830-40. 9.25" in diameter. *Courtesy of James & Elizabeth Dunn, Bittersweet Antiques.* $85-90.

Ne Plus platter by Thomas Fell, c. 1845. 17.75" x 14.25" *Courtesy of James & Elizabeth Dunn, Bittersweet Antiques.* $425-475.

Marks

This pottery used both impressed and printed marks including an anchor mark. Manufacturer's marks include "F", "FELL", "FELL & CO.", "F. & CO.", "T.F. & CO.", and "T. FELL & CO."

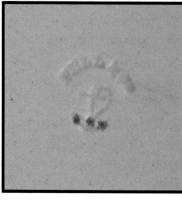

Thomas Fell, St. Peter's Pottery, Newcastle upon Tyne, Northumberland, 1817-90. Impressed Fell & Co. manufacturer's mark and anchor in use from c. 1830 to 1890. *Courtesy of James & Elizabeth Dunn, Bittersweet Antiques.*

Printed Thomas Fell "T.F. & Co." manufacturer's mark in use from c. 1830 to 1890. *Courtesy of James & Elizabeth Dunn, Bittersweet Antiques.*

Jacob Furnival & Company

Jacob Furnival & Company, the predecessor of Thomas Furnival & Sons was in business in Cobridge from c. 1845 to 1870. The company produced hard-bodied earthenwares for the export market including the Romantic Staffordshire Castle Scenery series.

Series and Views

Castle Scenery

A series of views shown here in light blue, featuring pillared arches, people in the foreground, and a castle across a lake in the background. Medallions in the border display views of their own.

Castle Scenery wash pitcher and supper plate by Jacob Furnival. Pitcher: 11" high; supper plate: 9" in diameter. *Courtesy of L.B. Gaignault.* Wash pitcher: $175-190; supper plate: $45-50.

Marks

Jacob Furnival & Company employed several printed marks with the initials "J F & CO." and the pattern name from c. 1845-1870.

Glamorgan Pottery Company (Baker, Bevans & Irwin)

Baker, Bevans & Irwin produced earthenware ceramics at the Glamorgan Pottery, Swansea, Wales, from 1813 to 1838. The firms produced the Romantic Staffordshire view Free Trade.

Series and Views

Free Trade

Free Trade sauce tureen underplate by Glamorgan Pottery Company (Baker, Bevans & Irwin), 1831- c. 1838. 8" wide. *Courtesy of L.B. Gaignault.* $50-55.

Marks

Manufacturer's marks found on this pottery's wares include the initials "B.B. & Co." or "G.P. Co." for Glamorgan Pottery Company. These marks were in use from 1813 to 1838.

Thomas Godwin

From 1809 to 1834 Thomas and Benjamin Godwin operated the New Wharf and New Basin potteries, producing creamwares and earthenwares. From 1834 to 1854 Thomas Godwin worked alone, producing transfer printed wares. With the increasing diversity in colors available for transfer printing, Godwin's export trade with America rose and the quality of his wares improved over the years. This is evident from his romantic series of views entitled William Penn's Treaty.

Series and Views

William Penn's Treaty

William Penn's Treaty side plate by Thomas Godwin, c. 1835. 7.25" in diameter. *Courtesy of James & Elizabeth Dunn, Bittersweet Antiques.* $100-110.

William Penn's Treaty supper plate by Thomas Godwin, c. 1835. 9.5" in diameter. *Courtesy of James & Elizabeth Dunn, Bittersweet Antiques.* $190-210.

William Penn's Treaty luncheon plate by Thomas Godwin, c. 1830s. 8.25" in diameter. *Courtesy of James & Elizabeth Dunn, Bittersweet Antiques.* $95-105.

William Penn's Treaty dinner plate by Thomas Godwin, c. 1840. 10.75" in diameter. *Courtesy of James & Elizabeth Dunn, Bittersweet Antiques.* $210-230.

William Penn's Treaty dinner plate by Thomas Godwin. 10.75" in diameter. *Courtesy of L.B. Gaignault.* $125-135.

Marks

Thomas Godwin used a variety of impressed or printed marks including a "T. G." initial mark, several marks with the name of the firm, the town and/or the body material. The printed mark present on the back of The Capitol, Washington plate reads OPAQUE CHINA, T GODWIN, WHARF (for New Wharf) and features a less-than-majestic British lion in the coat of arms.

Thomas Godwin, Canal Works, Navigation Road, Burslem, printed "T.G." manufacturer's mark in use from 1834 to 1854. *Courtesy of James & Elizabeth Dunn, Bittersweet Antiques.*

Thomas Goodfellow

Thomas Goodfellow operated the Phoenix Works in Tunstall from 1828 to 1859, producing earthenwares. His contributions to Romantic Staffordshire include Alleghany and Colonna.

Series and Views

Alleghany

Above and right: **Alleghany** platter by Thomas Goodfellow. 13.5" x 10.5". *Courtesy of L.B. Gaignault.* $200-220.

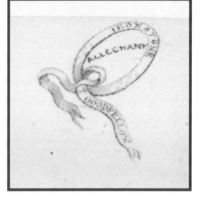

Colonna

Colonna covered vegetable dish by Thomas Goodfellow. 11.5" high. *Courtesy of L.B. Gaignault.* $125-135.

Versailles

Above and right: **Versailles** supper plate, possibly by John Goodwin. 9.75" in diameter. *Courtesy of L.B. Gaignault.* $75-80.

Marks

Thomas Goodfellow used a printed "T. GOODFELLOW" manufacturer's mark in a garter. The name of the view appears in the garter's center.

Goodwin & Ellis

This firm briefly produced earthenwares from Flint Street, Lane End, from c. 1839 to 1840. The firm had previously been Goodwin & Harris. This pottery produced the romantic print Peruvian Hunters.

Series and Views

Peruvian Hunters

There were several scenes produced with this title.

Below and left: **Peruvian Hunters** platter by Goodwin & Ellis. 17.5" x 14.5". *Courtesy of L.B. Gaignault.* $275-300.

Marks

The printed manufacturer's mark includes the firm's initials "G. & E." along with the name of the view.

John Hall & Sons

This firm carried on after the dissolution of a partnership with Ralph Hall in 1822. Earthenwares were produced at the Sytch Pottery of Burslem, from 1814 to 1832. The firm's views and series of views include Antiquities, Oriental Scenery, and Quadrupeds.

Series and Views

Antiquities

Quadrupeds Series

A series of animal images including: Antelope; Camel; Deer; Dog; Dog and rabbit; Fox; Horse and colt; Hyena; Lion; Moose and Hunter; Otter; Polar Bear; Rabbit and Hunter; Rhinoceros; and Wolverine.

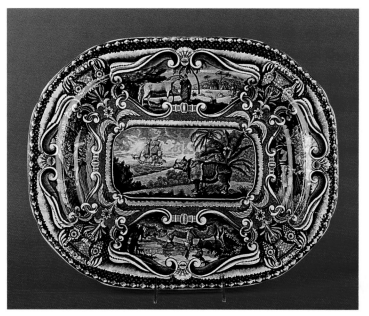

Quadrupeds Series Rhinoceros platter by John Hall. 17" x 13.5". *Courtesy of Dora Landey.*

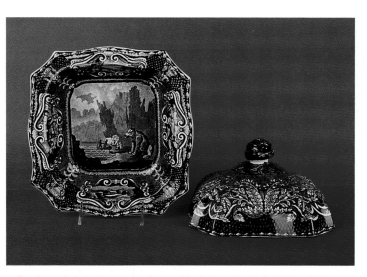

Quadrupeds Polar Bear covered vegetable dish by John Hall. 9.75" x 7" high. *Courtesy of Dora Landey.*

Above and right: **Antiquities** dinner plate by John Hall & Sons. 10" in diameter. *Courtesy of L.B. Gaignault.* $50-55.

Quadrupeds Lion dinner plate by John Hall. 10" in diameter. *Courtesy of Dora Landey.*

Quadrupeds Antelope saucer by John Hall. 7.5" in diameter. *Courtesy of Dora Landey.*

The words "& Sons" were added from c. 1822 to 1832. The previous mark was a simple "I. Hall" in use from 1814 to 1822.

John Hall, Sytch Pottery, Burslem, printed "I. Hall" manufacturer's mark in use from 1814 to 1832. *Courtesy of Dora Landey.*

Ralph Hall & Company

Ralph Hall produced transfer printed earthenwares for the export market in America from 1822 to 1849 at Swan Bank, Tunstall, Staffordshire. In c. 1836 the company name was changed to Ralph Hall & Son. This did not last long apparently. In 1841 the name changed again, this time to Ralph Hall & Company.

Series and Views

Carolina

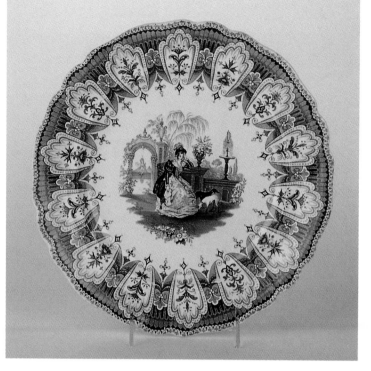

The Favorite dinner plate by Ralph Hall & Company, c. 1841. 10.75" in diameter. *Courtesy of James & Elizabeth Dunn, Bittersweet Antiques.* $85-90.

Left and above: **Carolina** plate by Ralph Hall, c. 1822-41. 8.75" in diameter. *Courtesy of James & Elizabeth Dunn, Bittersweet Antiques.* $75-80.

Opposite page:
Quadrupeds Fox basket by John Hall. 12" x 8.5" *Courtesy of Dora Landey.*

Italian Buildings

A series of romantic views depicting a variety of fanciful Italian buildings. Each scene shows two women in the foreground beneath a giant urn.

Italian Buildings pie plate by Ralph Hall. 6.75" in diameter. *Courtesy of L.B. Gaignault.* $50-55.

Parisian Chateau

A series of romantic French chateaux patterns encircled by a flower and scroll border. These images have been found printed in blue, green, sepia, pink, purple, and black.

Sardinia

Sardinia pitcher by Ralph Hall, c. 1840s. 8" high. *Courtesy of James & Elizabeth Dunn, Bittersweet Antiques.* $175-195.

Sheltered Peasants

Sheltered Peasants luncheon plate by Ralph Hall. 8.5" in diameter. *Courtesy of L.B. Gaignault.* $100-110.

Left: **Parisian Chateau** dinner plate by Ralph Hall, c. 1822. 10" in diameter. *Courtesy of James & Elizabeth Dunn, Bittersweet Antiques.* $50-55.

Singanese

Robert Hamilton produced blue printed earthenwares at Stoke, from 1811 to 1826.

Series and Views

Ruined Castle and Bridge

Above and left: **Singanese** egg platter by Ralph Hall & Company and **Tippecanoe** supper plate by John Wedg Wood. 10" x 7" platter, 9.5" diameter plate. *Courtesy of L.B. Gaignault.* Platter: $75-80; supper plate: $60-65.

Marks

Ralph Hall employed several printed marks over the years. R. Hall is the constant among them. In c. 1836 the company mark changed from "R. HALL" to "R. HALL & SON." From 1841-1849 the mark changed again, this time to "R. HALL & CO." or "R H & CO."

Ruined Castle and Bridge small pitcher by Hamilton. 6" high x 6". *Courtesy of Dora Landey.*

Marks

Robert Hamilton employed an impressed "HAMILTON / STOKE" mark.

Ralph Hall & Company, Swan Bank, Tunstall, printed "R. Hall & Co." manufacturer's mark in use from 1841 to 1849. *Courtesy of James & Elizabeth Dunn, Bittersweet Antiques.*

Ralph Hall, Swan Bank, Tunstall, 1822-49, printed "R. HALL" manufacturer's mark in use from 1822 to 1841. *Courtesy of James & Elizabeth Dunn, Bittersweet Antiques.*

Sampson Hancock & Company

Sampson Hancock produced earthenwares at the Bridge Works, Stoke, from 1858 to 1937.

Series and Views

Albion

Above and right: **Albion** supper plate by Sampson Hancock & Company. 9.25" in diameter. *Courtesy of L.B. Gaignault.* $50-55.

Marks

This firm used printed manufacturer's marks employing the company's initials "S.H." and the name "S. HANCOCK."

J. Harris

One light blue Sèvres view marked "I. Harris" has been found and is presented here.

Series and Views

Sèvres

Sèvres platter by I. Harris. 12.5" x 9.5". *Courtesy of L.B. Gaignault.* $175-190.

C. & W.K. Harvey

This firm, as well as Charles Harvey & Sons, produced earthenwares and china at Stafford Street, Charles Street, Chancery Lane, Longton, from 1835 to 1853. The Stafford Street works were continued by Holland & Green.

Series and Views

Ailanthus

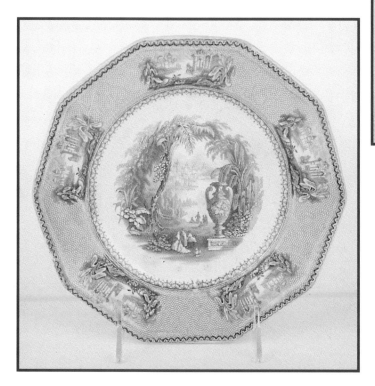

Above and left: **Ailanthus**
luncheon plate by C. & W.K.
Harvey. 8" in diameter.
Courtesy of L.B. Gaignault.
$50-55.

Gothic Temple

Above and right: **Gothic Temple** luncheon soup plate by C. & W.K. Harvey. 9"
in diameter. *Courtesy of L.B. Gaignault.* $65-70.

Marks

This pottery used printed initial marks including a nondescript "H." and a more informative "C. & W.K. H." mark. In each case, the name of the view is included in the mark.

John Hawley

John Hawley & Company produced earthenwares at Foley Pottery in Foley, from 1842 to 1887. The romantic Valetta view is shown here in light blue.

Series and Views

Valetta

Above and right: **Valetta** dinner plate by J.H. Hawley. 10.25" in diameter. *Courtesy of L.B. Gaignault.* $85-90.

Marks

The firm used both impressed and printed marks. The printed mark includes the "J. Hawley" name and the name of the view.

Joseph Heath & Company

Joseph Heath & Company operated out of the Newfield Pottery, Tunstall, Staffordshire, from 1828 to 1841 producing a variety of earthenwares. Transfer printed colors tend toward the lighter shades and include a light blue, brown, purple, pink, and black.

Series and Views

Amaryllis

Above and right: **Amaryllis** dinner soup plate by Joseph Heath & Company, c. 1835. 10" in diameter. *Courtesy of James & Elizabeth Dunn, Bittersweet Antiques.* $95-105.

Cintra open vegetable dish by Joseph Heath & Company. 9.5" x 7". *Courtesy of L.B. Gaignault.* $100-110.

Asia Displayed dinner plate by Joseph Heath & Company, c. 1830. 10.25" in diameter. *Courtesy of James & Elizabeth Dunn, Bittersweet Antiques.* $95-105.

Above and right: **Belvoir** side plate by Joseph Heath. 7.5" in diameter. *Courtesy of L.B. Gaignault.* $35-40.

Italian Villas

A romantic series of flowery patterns printed in light blue. These patterns were also printed in pink and purple.

Above and left: **Italian Villas** dinner soup plate by Joseph Heath, c. 1838. 10" in diameter. *Courtesy of James & Elizabeth Dunn, Bittersweet Antiques.* $95-105.

Italian Villas soup bowl by Joseph Heath, c. 1838-41. 8.75" in diameter. *Courtesy of James & Elizabeth Dunn, Bittersweet Antiques.* $55-60.

Above and left: **Lombardy** dinner plate by Joseph Heath & Company, 1828-1841. 10.5" in diameter. *Courtesy of L.B. Gaignault.* $75-85.

Military Sketches supper plate by Joseph Heath & Company. 9.5" in diameter. *Courtesy of L.B. Gaignault.* $75-80.

Milanese Pavillions

Milanese Pavillions supper plate by Joseph Heath & Company, c. 1828-41. 9" in diameter. *Courtesy of James & Elizabeth Dunn, Bittersweet Antiques.* $60-65.

Monterey

Above and left: **Monterey** luncheon soup plate by Joseph Heath. 9" in diameter. *Courtesy of L.B. Gaignault.* $75-80.

Ontario Lake Scenery

A series of Canadian lake views that are identical to a Lake series by an unknown potter.

Ontario Lake Scenery coffee pot and open vegetable dish by Joseph Heath. 6" x 8" vegetable dish. *Courtesy of L.B. Gaignault.* Coffee pot: $250-275; open vegetable dish: $100-110.

Persian

Persian small platter by Joseph Heath and Company, c. 1828-41. 9.5" x 7.75".
Courtesy of James & Elizabeth Dunn, Bittersweet Antiques. $150-165.

Rural Scenery

Far right and right: **Rural Scenery** dinner plate by Joseph Heath & Company. 10.5" in diameter. *Courtesy of L.B. Gaignault.* $100-110.

Joseph Heath used several different printed marks over the years. These included "J. HEATH & CO.", "J. H. & CO.", and the initial J is frequently printed as an I to create a "I. H. & CO." mark.

Joseph Heath & Company, Newfield Pottery, Tunstall, printed "J.H. & Co." manufacturer's mark in use from 1828 to 1841. *Courtesy of James & Elizabeth Dunn, Bittersweet Antiques.*

Henshall, Williamson & Company

This was one of the smaller firms operating out of Longport, Staffordshire. It went through several partnerships, including Henshall & Company (c. 1795), Henshall, Williamson & Clowes (c. 1790-1795), and Henshall, Williamson & Company (c. 1802-1828). Complicating the situation is the manufacturer's mark presented here which reads "Henshall and Williamson." Much of the confusion originates in the habit of this small firm (common to many of its counterparts with limited size and stature) not to mark its wares. The recorded marks to date are mostly for Henshall & Company. The firm produced dark and medium blue transfer prints for the American and the English and European markets. The wares produced were quality products.

Series and Views

Gothic Scenery

Far right and right: **Gothic Scenery** dinner plate by Henshall & Williamson. 10.25" in diameter. *Courtesy of L.B. Gaignault.* $90-100.

Henshall, Williamson & Company have provided this "Henshall and Williamson" printed manufacturer's mark, complete with the "Gothic Scenery" name of the romantic view.

Herculaneum Pottery & Company

Herculaneum Pottery & Company was operated by a variety of individuals including Messrs. Samuel Worthington, Humble & Holland and others. The pottery operated out of Liverpool, Lancashire, from c. 1793 to 1841, producing a variety of earthenwares and porcelains. Romantic Staffordshire series produced by the firm include Archery, the Cherub Medallion Border Series, and the India Series.

Series and Views

Archery

Opposite page: **Archery** teapot by Herculaneum Pottery and Company, c. 1835. 7" high x 9.5" wide. *Courtesy of James & Elizabeth Dunn, Bittersweet Antiques.* $145-160.

Marks

Impressed and printed marks feature the name "HERCULANEUM".

Archery side plate by Herculaneum Pottery Company. 8" in diameter. *Courtesy of L.B. Gaignault.* $70-75.

John Holland

John Holland briefly produced earthenwares at Clay Hills Pottery in Tunstall from 1852 to 1854. Among them was this classical scene entitled Carrara.

Series and Views

Carrara

Above and right: **Carrara** pie plate by John Holland. 6.75" in diameter. *Courtesy of L.B. Gaignault.* $35-40.

Hulse, Nixon & Adderly

This firm operated out of the Daisy Bank Works in Longton, from 1853 to 1868. Among their eathenwares was this romantic series entitled Mycenae.

Series and Views

Mycene

This series features a prominent vase in the foreground, water and classical structures in the background, and a border including medallions with shells and floral sprays along with women alternately engaged in harp playing or bust sculpting.

Mycene luncheon soup plate, cup and saucer by Hulse, Nixon & Adderly. 9.5" diameter soup plate; 3.5" diameter cup; 6" diameter saucer. *Courtesy of L.B. Gaignault.* Luncheon soup plate: $75-80; cup and saucer: $50-55.

Thomas Ingleby & Company

This firm produced transfer printed earthenwares at High Street in Tunstall briefly from c. 1834 to 1835.

Marks

The company used a printed "J. Holland" mark here along with the pattern name. The registration mark indicates a registry date of 1852.

Series and Views

Gothic Beauties

Above and left: **Gothic Beauties** bonbon dish by Thomas Ingleby & Company. 6.5" in diameter. *Courtesy of L.B. Gaignault.* $50-55.

Marks

The company's printed "T.I. & Co." mark is presented here. The name of the view is included with the mark.

Job & John Jackson

Job and John Jackson produced earthenwares from the Church Yard Works, Burslem, Staffordshire from 1831 to 1835. The Jacksons produced transfer printed wares in light blue, purple, sepia, pink, and black. Their borders were open and flowered in a manner typical for this period. Their wares were largely targeted to the American export trade.

Series and Views

Antelope

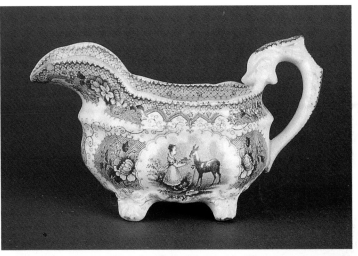

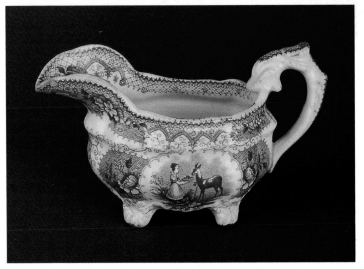

Above two: **Antelope** creamer by Job and John Jackson. 3.5" high by 6.5" wide. *Courtesy of James & Elizabeth Dunn, Bittersweet Antiques.* $40-45.

Asiatic Scenery

Asiatic Scenery luncheon plate by Job and John Jackson, c. 1831-35. 8" in diameter. *Courtesy of James & Elizabeth Dunn, Bittersweet Antiques.* $50-55.

Clyde Scenery dinner plate by Job & John Jackson,, c. 1831. 10.5" in diameter. *Courtesy of James & Elizabeth Dunn, Bittersweet Antiques.* $95-105.

Clyde Scenery

Clyde Scenery by Job & John Jackson, c. 1831. 10.25" in diameter. *Courtesy of James & Elizabeth Dunn, Bittersweet Antiques.* $90-100.

Clyde Scenery supper plate by Job and John Jackson, c. 1830s. 9.25" in diameter. *Courtesy of James & Elizabeth Dunn, Bittersweet Antiques.* $75-80.

Clyde Scenery side plate by Job & John Jackson, c. 1831. 7" in diameter. *Courtesy of James & Elizabeth Dunn, Bittersweet Antiques.* $50-55.

Clyde Scenery side plate by Job & John Jackson, c. 1831. 7" in diameter. *Courtesy of James & Elizabeth Dunn, Bittersweet Antiques.* $45-50.

A rare multi-colored **Clyde Scenery** dinner plate by Job & John Jackson, c. 1831. 10.5" in diameter. *Courtesy of James & Elizabeth Dunn, Bittersweet Antiques.* $135-145.

Clyde Scenery covered soup tureen by Job & John Jackson, c. 1831-35. 13" wide x 11" high. *Courtesy of James & Elizabeth Dunn, Bittersweet Antiques.* $750-825.

Left and above two: **Clyde Scenery** pitcher by Job and John Jackson, c. 1835. Note that the scenery goes all the way around the pitcher. 8" high. *Courtesy of James & Elizabeth Dunn, Bittersweet Antiques.* NP.

Florentine Villas

Temple scenes printed in a variety of colors and surrounded by a floral border.

Valencia

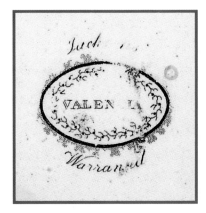

Above and right: **Florentine Villas** dinner soup plate by Job & John Jackson. 10.25" in diameter. *Courtesy of L.B. Gaignault.* $95-105.

Above and right: A very rare and desirable two colored **Valencia** plate by Job and John Jackson, c. 1831-35. 10" in diameter. *Courtesy of James & Elizabeth Dunn, Bittersweet Antiques.* $125-135.

Marks

Swiss Boy

Swiss Boy cup and saucer by Jackson's Warranted. *Courtesy of L.B. Gaignault.* $80-85.

The Jackson's used several printed and impressed marks. The common feature among them was the manufacturer's name presented as either "J. & J. JACKSON" or "JACKSON'S WARRANTED".

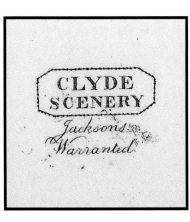

Job & John Jackson, Church Yard Works, Burslem, "JACKSON'S WARRANTED" printed manufacturer's mark in use from 1831 to 1835. *Courtesy of James & Elizabeth Dunn, Bittersweet Antiques.*

Elijah Jones

Elijah Jones produced transfer printed earthenwares from the Villa Pottery, Cobridge, from 1831 to 1839.

Series and Views

Denon's Egypt

Above and right: **Denon's Egypt** nappy plate by Elijah Jones. 8.5" in diameter. *Courtesy of L.B. Gaignault.* $150-165.

Marks

Elijah Jones used his printed initials "E.J." to identify his wares.

James Keeling

James Keeling operated out of New Street, Hanley, from c. 1790 to 1832. Mr. Keeling shared a predisposition with John Hall to use views from *Travels in Mesopotamia* by J.L. Buckingham (1828). (Coysh & Henrywood 1982, 200)

Series and Views

Views in Mesopotamia

A series of views taken from J.L. Buckingham's Travels in Mesopotamia and printed in black or blue. The identified view include:

Oriental Conversazione and Garden Entertainment; Tomb of Zobeida, Wife of Horoun-el-Rashid, the Caliph of Bagdad; Return from a Desert Excursion in Search of the Walls of Babylon; Turkish Coffee-House near the Bridge of Boats on the Tigris at Bagdad; A Fountain near Aleppo; and View of Birs Nimroud. (Coysh & Henrywood 1989, 206)

Above and right: **Views in Mesopotamia** dinner plate by James Keeling. 10.5" in diameter. *Courtesy of L.B. Gaignault.* $95-105.

John King Knight

This pottery produced transfer printed earthenwares at The Foley Potteries in Fenton, from 1846 to 1853. The firm was previously Knight, Elkin & Company.

Series and Views

Geneva

Above and right: **Geneva** supper plate by John King Knight. 9.5" in diameter. *Courtesy of L.B. Gaignault.* $75-80.

Marks

This pottery is known to use an "I.K. KNIGHT" mark coupled with "FOLEY". Shown here are both an impressed and printed mark featuring the British lion and unicorn crest and the manufacturer's initial mark "J.K.K."

Knight, Elkin & Company

The predecessor of John King Knight was also listed as Elkin & Knight. Their printed earthenwares were produced at The Foley Potteries, Fenton, from 1826 to 1846.

Series and Views

Hannibal Passing the Alps

Several variations of the central scene were created in this pattern. It was printed in blue, sepia, and red.

Above and left: **Hannibal Passing the Alps** dinner plate by Knight, Elkin & Company. 10.5" in diameter. *Courtesy of L.B. Gaignault.* $95-105.

Pennsylvania dinner plate by Knight, Elkin & Company, c. 1826-46. 10.5" in diameter. *Courtesy of James & Elizabeth Dunn, Bittersweet Antiques.* $110-120.

Marks

This firm used a printed "K.E. & Co." manufacturer's mark throughout this period.

Right: Knight, Elkin & Company, Foley Potteries, Fenton, 1826-46, printed "K.E. & Co." manufacturer's mark in use throughout this period. *Courtesy of James & Elizabeth Dunn, Bittersweet Antiques.*

Livesley, Powell & Company

Livesley Powell & Company produced earthenwares, including ironstone and china, at Old Hall Lane and Miles Bank, Hanley from 1851 to 1866. After 1866, the firm became Powell & Bishop.

Series and Views

Abbey

Above and right: **Abbey** supper plate by Livesley Powell & Company. 9.5" in diameter. *Courtesy of L.B. Gaignault.* $65-70.

Marks

The company used a printed "L.P. & Co." mark during this period. The mark includes both the "Ironstone" body name and the name of the view.

John Maddock & Sons

John Maddock & Sons operated out of Newcastle St. and Dale Hall in Burselm, from 1855 onward. The firm was previously known as J. Maddock.

Series and Views

Verano

Above two and left: **Verano** supper plate by John Maddock & Sons. 9.5" in diameter. *Courtesy of L.B. Gaignault.* $75-80.

Marks

The company used both a printed and impressed "MADDOCK" manufacturer's mark. The "Ironstone" body name is included along with the pattern name in the printed mark.

Manufacturer Unknown

It was common for smaller firms not to mark their wares. Either they had no name recognition and the mark would do them no good or their stay in business was too short to record any mark they did manage to create. These manufacturers produced a variety of views and dealt with a number of themes in their wares. These firms also frequently neglected to name their patterns, as will soon become apparent.

Series and Views

Above and right: **Adelaide's Bower** dinner plate, maker unknown. 10.5" in diameter. *Courtesy of James & Elizabeth Dunn, Bittersweet Antiques.* $95-105.

Acropolis supper plate, no manufacturer's mark. 9.25" in diameter. *Courtesy of L.B. Gaignault.* $65-70.

Acropolis side plate, manufacturer unknown. 7" in diameter. *Courtesy of James & Elizabeth Dunn, Bittersweet Antiques.* $45-50.

Adelaide's Bower wash basin, manufacturer unknown, c. 1835. 13" in diameter x 4" high. *Courtesy of James & Elizabeth Dunn, Bittersweet Antiques.* $400-440.

"Apollo" bowl, manufacturer unknown. 6" in diameter. *Courtesy of L.B. Gaignault.* $20-22.

Adelaide's Bower covered vegetable dish, manufacturer unknown, c. 1835. 6" high x 12.5" wide. *Courtesy of James & Elizabeth Dunn, Bittersweet Antiques.* $335-370.

Arcadia supper plate, manufacturer unknown, marked "F. & W." Geoffrey Godden states that this mark is found on mid-nineteenth century earthenwares but that it does not relate to any Staffordshire firm of the period. He believes F.

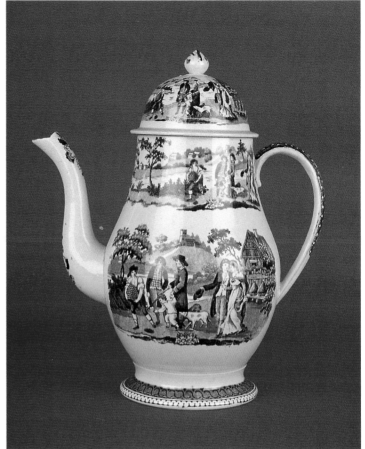

The Beemaster coffee pot, manufacturer unknown. 12" high by 9" *Courtesy of Dora Landey.*

Above and right: Asiatic Plants supper plate, manufacturer unknown, c. 1830-40. 9.5" in diameter. *Courtesy of James & Elizabeth Dunn, Bittersweet Antiques.* $80-85.

"Bird on Fountain" covered vegetable dish, manufacturer unknown. 9.5" x 12". *Courtesy of L.B. Gaignault.* $100-110.

Botanical Beauties platter, manufacturer unknown, c. 1840. 15.75" x 12.5" *Courtesy of James & Elizabeth Dunn, Bittersweet Antiques.* $375-415.

Bower supper plate, manufacturer unknown. 9" in diameter. *Courtesy of L.B. Gaignault.* $50-55.

Boy Piping covered soup tureen, manufacturer unknown. 14" x 9" high. *Courtesy of Dora Landey.*

British Cattle hor d'oeurvres dish, manufacturer unidentified but bearing a "B.B. & B" mark. 5" high, 13" wide handle to handle. *Courtesy of Lisa Worden: Sloane Square Antiques.* $495-550.

Above and right: **Brooklyn** dinner plate by either Skinner & Walker or Wedgwood. 10.5" in diameter. *Courtesy of L.B. Gaignault.* $110-120.

Above and right: **Chiang Nan** pattern in a **Beauties of China** series dinner plate, manufacturer unknown. 10.5" in diameter. *Courtesy of L.B. Gaignault.* NP, this piece is unique.

Canova dinner plate, manufacturer unknown, c. 1835. 10.5" in diameter. *Courtesy of James & Elizabeth Dunn, Bittersweet Antiques.* $95-105.

"Classical Urns & Vases" oval covered vegetable dish, no manufacturer's mark. 13.5" x 9" x 7.5" high. *Courtesy of L.B. Gaignault.* $120-130.

Crystal Palace dinner plate, manufacturer unknown. 10.25" in diameter. *Courtesy of L.B. Gaignault.* $90-100.

Above, right and top right: **"David Parry Colebrook"** is printed on this unidentified fishing scene pitcher, manufacturer unknown. 7.5" high x 7.5". *Courtesy of Dora Landey.*

Ekorie Birds teapot, manufacturer unknown. 7" high. *Courtesy of James & Elizabeth Dunn, Bittersweet Antiques.* $400-440.

Family and Mule large mug by an unknown manufacturer. 6" high x 4.25" in diameter. *Courtesy of Dora Landey.*

Fisherman's Hut platter, manufacturer unknown. 19" x 14.5". *Courtesy of Dora Landey.*

Fisherman's Hut reticulated chestnut holder and undertray, manufacturer unknown. 12" x 4" high. *Courtesy of Dora Landey.*

Fruit Basket and **Fruit and Flowers** children's covered sugar bowls and creamers, manufacturer unknown. 3" high x 5" wide. *Courtesy of James & Elizabeth Dunn, Bittersweet Antiques.* NP.

A closer look at the **Fruit and Flowers** child's covered sugar bowl and creamer, manufacturer unknown. 3" high x 5" wide. *Courtesy of James & Elizabeth Dunn, Bittersweet Antiques.* NP.

Fruit and Flowers platter, manufacturer unknown. 14.75" x 11.75" *Courtesy of Dora Landey.* NP

Fruit and Flowers platter, manufacturer unknown. 18.5" x 15" *Courtesy of Dora Landey.* NP

Fruit and Flowers dinner plate, manufacturer unknown. 10" in diameter. *Courtesy of Dora Landey.* NP

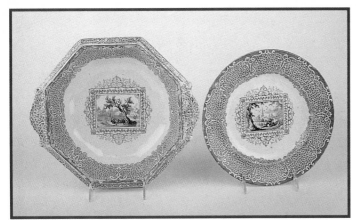

Above and right: **Gipsy** octagonal soup tureen base and supper plate, manufacturer unknown. Tureen: 11.5" in diameter. *Courtesy of L.B. Gaignault.* Tureen base: $120-130; supper plate: $75-80.

"Greek Patterns" vegetable dish, manufacturer unknown, possibly by Spode. 9" x 11.5". *Courtesy of L.B. Gaignault.* $150-165.

"GOD is altogether LOVELY" printed on a mug with an unidentified Oriental pattern, manufacturer unknown. 4" x 5" high. *Courtesy of Dora Landey.*

Gravesend black transfer printed creamer, manufacturer unknown, c. 1830s. 4.5" high x 7" wide. *Courtesy of James & Elizabeth Dunn, Bittersweet Antiques.* $115-125.

Above and left: **Grecian Scenery** dinner plate, manufacturer unknown, marked "Stone China". 10.25" in diameter. *Courtesy of L.B. Gaignault.* $75-80.

Harvest Scenery pitcher, no manufacturer's mark, c. 1831. 8" high, 6.25" high to lip. *Courtesy of James & Elizabeth Dunn, Bittersweet Antiques.* $325-360.

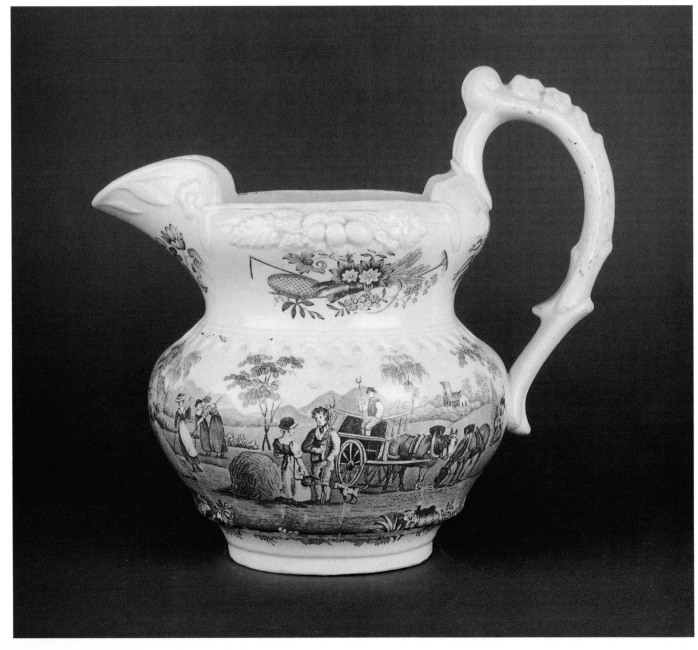

Hop Pickers covered soup tureen with underplate, manufacturer unknown. 13" x 9" high. *Courtesy of Dora Landey.*

Imperial Flowers covered vegetable dish with an flower finial, manufacturer unknown, c. 1830. 7" high x 12" wide. *Courtesy of James & Elizabeth Dunn, Bittersweet Antiques.* $335-365.

Above and right: **Lawrence** luncheon soup plate, marked "S" — manufacturer unidentified. 9.75" in diameter. *Courtesy of L.B. Gaignault.* $50-55.

Above and left: **Locarno** dinner plate, manufacturer unidentified. 10.5" in diameter. *Courtesy of L.B. Gaignault.* $75-80.

Lousanne Villa luncheon plate, manufacturer unknown, c. 1835-50. 8" in diameter. *Courtesy of James & Elizabeth Dunn, Bittersweet Antiques.* $45-50.

The March, part of an Arabian Sketches series, supper plate, possibly by William Hackwood, c. 1827-43. 9" in diameter. *Courtesy of James & Elizabeth Dunn, Bittersweet Antiques.* $75-80.

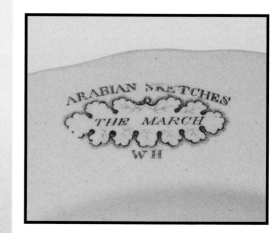

Printed W.H. manufacturer's mark, possibly the mark of William Hackwood, Eastwood, Hanley, 1827-43. *Courtesy of James & Elizabeth Dunn, Bittersweet*

"M. Ainsley" unidentified pattern three piece smoker's set, manufacturer unknown, c. 1835. The handles are carved cameo faces. This set includes a tray, tobacco jar, and combination lid and candlestick holder. 5.5" in diameter, 9" high. *Courtesy of James & Elizabeth Dunn, Bittersweet Antiques.* $515-565.

Milanese dinner plate, manufacturer unknown, c. 1830. 10" in diameter. *Courtesy of James & Elizabeth Dunn, Bittersweet Antiques.* $95-105.

Morea platter, manufacturer unknown, c. 1830-40. 19.5" x 14.5" *Courtesy of James & Elizabeth Dunn, Bittersweet Antiques.* $400-440.

"Organ Grinder" handleless child's cup, unidentified manufacturer — possibly Machin & Potts. 2.75" in diameter. *Courtesy of L.B. Gaignault.* $50-55.

Milanese Scenery dinner plate, manufacturer unknown, c. 1840. 10.75" in diameter. *Courtesy of James & Elizabeth Dunn, Bittersweet Antiques.* $95-105.

"Milkmaid" covered sugar with an unmatched lid, manufacturer unknown but possibly by Thomas Rathbone & Company. *Courtesy of L.B. Gaignault.* $95-105.

Above and right: **Oriental Barge** dinner plate, manufacturer unidentified. 10.25" in diameter. *Courtesy of M. R. Markowitz.* $75-80.

Palmyra (or Ionic, these pieces are never marked) small waste bowl and coffee cann, manufacturer unknown. 5" diameter waste bowl; 3.25" diameter cann. *Courtesy of L.B. Gaignault.* Waste bowl: $60-65; coffee can: $75-80.

Pagoda sauce tureen with undertray, no ladle, manufacturer unknown, c. 1830. Sauce tureen: 6.5" high x 8" wide. Underplate: 9" x 6.75" *Courtesy of James & Elizabeth Dunn, Bittersweet Antiques.* $265-290.

Pastoral cup and cup plate, manufacturer unknown. *Courtesy of Dora Landey.* $195-215 set.

Scroll platter, the manufacturer of the printed "B" mark is unknown, c. 1830s. 14.5" x 12". *Courtesy of James & Elizabeth Dunn, Bittersweet Antiques.* $360-395.

Primrose cup and saucer, manufacturer unknown, c. 1830-45. Cup: 4" wide x 2.5" high; saucer: 5.75" in diameter. *Courtesy of James & Elizabeth Dunn, Bittersweet Antiques.* $60-65 cup and saucer set.

Shannon supper plate, unidentified manufacturer. 9.25" in diameter. *Courtesy of L.B. Gaignault.* $75-80.

Above and below: Sicilian Beauties covered sauce tureen, manufacturer unknown, c. 1820. 6.5" high x 8" wide. *Courtesy of James & Elizabeth Dunn, Bittersweet Antiques.* $320-350.

The Son of Righteousness luncheon plate, manufacturer unknown. 8" in diameter. *Courtesy of James & Elizabeth Dunn, Bittersweet Antiques.* NP.

An unidentified pattern dinner soup plate by an unidentified manufacturer. 10.5" in diameter. *Courtesy of James & Elizabeth Dunn, Bittersweet Antiques.* $95-105.

An unidentified Dragon design with flowers on a dinner plate, manufacturer unknown. *Courtesy of James & Elizabeth Dunn, Bittersweet Antiques.* 10.5" in diameter. $95-105.

Right: A rare wash basin with an unidentified multi-color pattern by and unknown manufacturer. (Staffordshire multi color wash bowl). 13" in diameter, 4" deep. *Courtesy of James & Elizabeth Dunn, Bittersweet Antiques.* $400-440.

Above and right: An unidentified pattern side plate which has an impressed anchor mark on the back which may belong to Davenport. 7" in diameter. *Courtesy of James & Elizabeth Dunn, Bittersweet Antiques.* $45-50.

An unidentified pattern, possibly "Holy Bible," adorns this water pitcher, manufacturer unknown, c. 1830. 10" high. *Courtesy of James & Elizabeth Dunn, Bittersweet Antiques.* $325-355.

This coffee pot is decorated with an unidentified black transfer printed pattern, manufacturer unknown, c. 1840. 9.5" high. *Courtesy of James & Elizabeth Dunn, Bittersweet Antiques.* $325-355.

An unidentified classical pattern decorates this coffee pot, manufacturer unknown, c. 1830-40. 12" high. *Courtesy of James & Elizabeth Dunn, Bittersweet Antiques.* $500-550.

Opposite page: An unidentified floral pattern pitcher, manufacturer unknown, c. 1830s. 8" high. *Courtesy of James & Elizabeth Dunn, Bittersweet Antiques.* $370-400.

An unidentified pattern milk pitcher, manufacturer unknown, c. 1830-50. 6.25" high. *Courtesy of James & Elizabeth Dunn, Bittersweet Antiques.* $120-130.

An unidentified pattern mug, manufacturer unknown, c. 1840-60. 4.25" high x 4" high. *Courtesy of James & Elizabeth Dunn, Bittersweet Antiques.* $130-140.

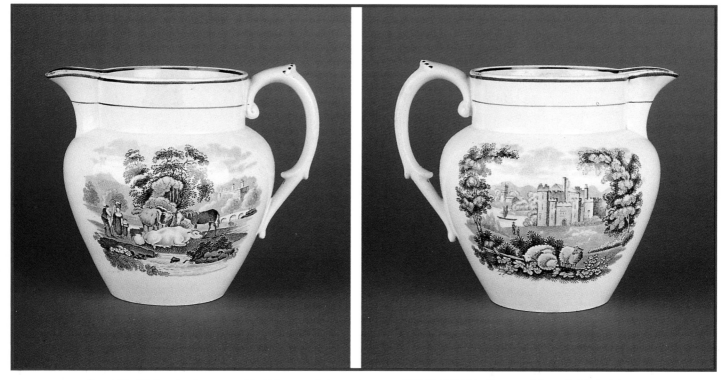

Two unidentified rural patterns grace this pitcher, manufacturer unknown, c. 1820-30. 5.5" high. *Courtesy of James & Elizabeth Dunn, Bittersweet Antiques.* $120-130.

An unidentified floral pattern water pitcher, manufacturer unknown, c. 1840s. 6.5" high. *Courtesy of James & Elizabeth Dunn, Bittersweet Antiques.* $180-200 .

An unidentified floral pattern covered sugar, manufacturer unknown, c. 1830s. 6" wide x 6" high. *Courtesy of James & Elizabeth Dunn, Bittersweet Antiques.* $120-130.

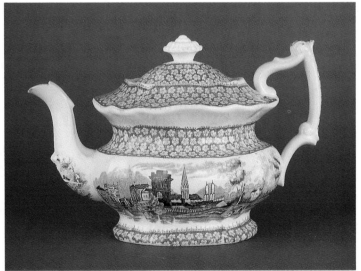

An unidentified city view with a central cathedral adorns this teapot, manufacturer unknown, c. 1840s. This is a rare piece. 7" high x 9.5" wide. *Courtesy of James & Elizabeth Dunn, Bittersweet Antiques.* $340-375.

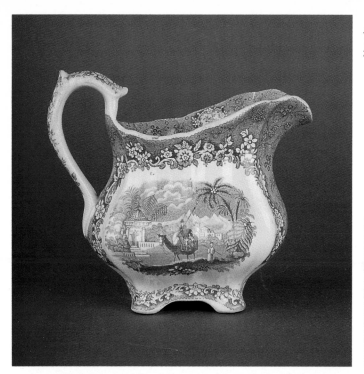

An unidentified Middle Eastern scene on a creamer, manufacturer unknown, c. 1830s. 4.5" high. *Courtesy of James & Elizabeth Dunn, Bittersweet Antiques.* $140-155.

Above, left and below: An unidentified pattern partial child's tea set, manufacturer unknown, c. 1860-70. Child's teapot: 6" high; creamer: 3.75" high; sugar bowl: 5.25" high; tea cups: 2" high x 3" in diameter; saucers: 5" in diameter. *Courtesy of James & Elizabeth Dunn, Bittersweet Antiques.* $600-660 set, waste bowl missing.

This unidentified pattern is similar in design to William Smith and Company's "Lion Antique." Side plate and waste bowl by an unidentified manufacturer. 7.25" diameter side plate; 6.25" diameter waste bowl. *Courtesy of L.B. Gaignault.* $125-135 each.

Windsor Castle covered sugar bowl, manufacturer unknown, c. 1820-40. 6.5" high. *Courtesy of James & Elizabeth Dunn, Bittersweet Antiques.* $115-125.

Village Church small platter, manufacturer unknown, c. 1835-45. 10.75" x 8". *Courtesy of James & Elizabeth Dunn, Bittersweet Antiques.* $150-165.

Village Church bowl, manufacturer unknown, c. 1835-45. 4" high x 9" in diameter. *Courtesy of Dora Landey.*

Marple, Turner & Company

Marple, Turner & Company produced Romantic Staffordshire views including Athena (registered in 1852) and Holly.

Series and Views

Athena

Athena nut dish by Marple Turner & Company. *Courtesy of L.B. Gaignault.* $20-22.

Holly

Above and left: **Holly** side plate by Marple, Turner & Company. 7.5" in diameter. *Courtesy of L.B. Gaignault.* $35-40.

Marks

Marple, Turner & Company used a printed garter mark including the initials "M.T. & Co." The pattern name is included in the mark.

Charles James Mason & Company

This pottery produced their ironstone wares at the Patent Ironstone China Manufactory on Lane Delph, from 1829 to 1845. The company was formerly known as G.M. & C.J. Mason and later as C.J. Mason. Many of the patterns of the earlier firm were continued by Charles James Mason & Company.

Series and Views

Damascus

Above two: **Damascus** teapot in an unusual shape by Charles James Mason and Company,, c. 1840-50. 12" wide by 7" high. *Courtesy of James & Elizabeth Dunn, Bittersweet Antiques.* NP.

Napoleon Series

This series illustrated specific events in Napoleon's military career. The scenes include:

Napoleon (several scenes); Napoleon at the Battle of Austerlitz; Napoleon at the Battle of Marengo; Napoleon's Battles — Return from Elba; Napoleon's Battles — Revolt of Cairo.

Below: **Napoleon** platter by C.J. Mason & Company. This is one of several different Napoleon scenes from C.J. Mason & Company's Napoleon Series. 13.25" x 10.75" *Courtesy of James & Elizabeth Dunn, Bittersweet Antiques.* $350-385.

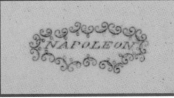

Left, above and right: **Napoleon** dinner plate and **Napoleon Battles** luncheon plate by Charles James Mason & Company. 10.5" blue dinner plate; 9" green luncheon plate. *Courtesy of L.B. Gaignault.* Dinner plate: $130-140; luncheon plate: $75-80.

Napoleon Battles platter by C.J. Mason and Company,, c. 1829-45. 15 3/4 in by 12.5" *Courtesy of James & Elizabeth Dunn, Bittersweet Antiques.* $350-385.

Marks

The familiar Mason's Patent Ironstone China manufacturer's mark continued to be used during this period, making it difficult to differentiate the wares of this firm with those of its predecessor. A variation of the Mason mark includes the word "Improved" around 1840.

Charles James Mason & Company, Patent Ironstone China Manufactory, Lane Delph, printed manufacturer's mark in use from 1829 to 1845. *Courtesy of James & Elizabeth Dunn, Bittersweet Antiques.*

T. J. & J. Mayer

Thomas, John & Joseph Mayer operated out of the Furlong Works and Dale Hall Pottery in Burslem from 1843 to 1855. The company produced earthenware, china, Parian, and other wares. The firm exhibited their quality wares at international exhibitions in 1851, 1853, and 1855. Their wares were highly regarded in their day. This company produced a variety of romantic patterns, all falling under the Copyright Law of 1842.

Baronial Halls

This series included costumed people positioned before a number of different buildings. These scenes decorated dinner and tea wares and were printed in light blue.

Above and right: **Baronial Halls** platter by T.J. & J. Mayer. 18" x 14". *Courtesy of L.B. Gaignault.* $300-330.

118

Florentine

Garden Scenery

A series of romantic scenes printed in light blue.

Above, right and above right: **Garden Scenery** large chamber pot by T.J. & J. Mayer. *Courtesy of L.B. Gaignault.* $300-330.

The Gem

The Gem large saucer by T.J. & J. Mayer. 6.5" in diameter. *Courtesy of L.B. Gaignault.* $30-35.

Non Pareil

A romantic series of prints featuring a variety of mosques or temples with people in the foreground. These patterns were printed in blue, green, brown, and sepia.

Non Pareil wash basin and pitcher by T.J. & J. Mayer, c. 1837. This set has a very rare and unusual body shape. Pitcher: 10" high; wash bowl: 12" in diameter x 4" high. *Courtesy of James & Elizabeth Dunn, Bittersweet Antiques.* $500-550 set.

Thomas Mayer

Thomas Mayer produced earthenwares first at the Cliff Bank Works, Stoke, Staffordshire from c. 1826 to 1835 and from Brook Street, Longport, Staffordshire from c. 1826 to 1838. Thomas Mayer exported his blue transfer printed wares extensively to the United States.

Series and Views

Abbey Ruins

Above and right: **Rhône Scenery** supper plate by T.J. & J. Mayer, 1843-1855. 9.75" in diameter. *Courtesy of L.B. Gaignault.* $60-65.

Marks

This company used the printed manufacturer's mark "T.J. & J. Mayer" throughout their years of production.

Above and right: **Abbey Ruins** dinner plate by T. Mayer, Longport, c. 1836-38. 10.5" in diameter. *Courtesy of James & Elizabeth Dunn, Bittersweet Antiques.* $95-105.

"T.J. & J. Mayer" printed manufacturer's mark. *Courtesy of James & Elizabeth Dunn, Bittersweet Antiques.*

Abbey Ruins teapot by Thomas Mayer, c. 1836-38. 8" high. *Courtesy of James & Elizabeth Dunn, Bittersweet Antiques.* $200-220.

Above and below: **Abbey Ruins** covered vegetable dish by Thomas Mayer, c. 1836-38. 12.5" long x 9" wide. *Courtesy of James & Elizabeth Dunn, Bittersweet Antiques.* $380-420.

Abbey Ruins possible muffineer/pepper pot/sander (a sander held sand when writing with a quill pen and is very rare) by Thomas Mayer, c. 1836-38. *Courtesy of James & Elizabeth Dunn, Bittersweet Antiques.* $125-135.

Canova

    A series of patterns, all of which contain a large urn. These patterns decorated both tea and dinner services.

Canova platter by T. Mayer, c. 1835. 15.5" x 13.25" *Courtesy of James & Elizabeth Dunn, Bittersweet Antiques.* $350-385.

Below: **Canova** platter by Thomas Mayer, c. 1830s. 20.25" x 16.75" *Courtesy of James & Elizabeth Dunn, Bittersweet Antiques.* $490-540.

Canova dinner plate by Thomas Mayer, c. 1835. 10.5" in diameter. *Courtesy of James & Elizabeth Dunn, Bittersweet Antiques.* $95-105.

Canova water pitcher by Thomas Mayer, c. 1835. 7" high. *Courtesy of James & Elizabeth Dunn, Bittersweet Antiques.* $100-110.

Canova teapot by Thomas Mayer, c. 1830. 10" wide x 6.5" high. *Courtesy of James & Elizabeth Dunn, Bittersweet Antiques.* $290-320.

Canova handleless cup and cup plate (the saucer is missing) by Thomas Mayer. Cup: 4" in diameter x 2.25" high; cup plate: 5" in diameter. *Courtesy of James & Elizabeth Dunn, Bittersweet Antiques.* NP.

Canova covered sugar bowl by Thomas Mayer. 6" high. *Courtesy of James & Elizabeth Dunn, Bittersweet Antiques.* $125-135.

A very rare multi-colored **Canova** pattern wash pitcher by Thomas Mayer, c. 1835. 9.75" high. *Courtesy of James & Elizabeth Dunn, Bittersweet Antiques.* $600-660.

Gothic dome lid coffee pot by Thomas Mayer, c. 1825-35. 12.5" high. *Courtesy of James & Elizabeth Dunn, Bittersweet Antiques.* $600-660.

Mogul Scenery supper plate by Thomas Mayer, c. 1826-35. 9" in diameter. *Courtesy of James & Elizabeth Dunn, Bittersweet Antiques.* $55-60.

Mogul Scenery side plate by Thomas Mayer, c. 1826-35. 7.75" in diameter. *Courtesy of James & Elizabeth Dunn, Bittersweet Antiques.* $45-50

Mogul Scenery covered vegetable dish by Thomas Mayer, c. 1826-35. 12" wide x 6" high. *Courtesy of James & Elizabeth Dunn, Bittersweet Antiques.* $300-330.

A series of light blue, sepia, and black scenes including: Animal Prize Fight; Darting; The Discus; Spanish Bull Fight; Victors Crowned.

Above and right: **32** cream pitcher by Thomas Mayer. 4" high. *Courtesy of L.B. Gaignault.* $100-110.

Above and right: **The Discus** pattern (from the **Olympic Games** series) dinner plate by Thomas Mayer, c. 1826-35. 10.25" in diameter. *Courtesy of L.B. Gaignault.* $100-110.

Marks

The name "T. MAYER" is the common feature to several printed Mayer marks. The addition of "Stoke" to the name indicates the ware dates before 1836.

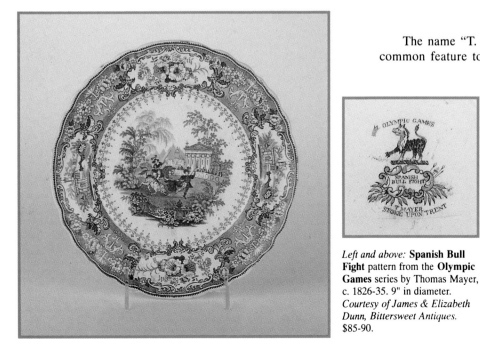

Left and above: **Spanish Bull Fight** pattern from the **Olympic Games** series by Thomas Mayer, c. 1826-35. 9" in diameter. *Courtesy of James & Elizabeth Dunn, Bittersweet Antiques.* $85-90.

Right: Thomas Mayer, Cliff Bank Works, Stoke, c. 1826-35, and Brook St., Longport, c. 1836-38, printed "T. Mayer Stoke Upon Trent" and impressed "T. Mayer Stoke" manufacturer's marks. The "Stoke" name in the mark indicates a date prior to 1836. *Courtesy of James & Elizabeth Dunn,*

The Meigh Family

Job Meigh built the Old Hall Pottery in Hanley in c. 1770, potting cream-colored and red earthenwares. The works ran uninterrupted in the family until 1861. Job Meigh took his son Charles into the business in around 1812 and the firm Job Meigh & Sons produced wares until 1834. The pottery traded under the name Charles Meigh from 1835-1849, producing the Romantic Staffordshire wares portrayed here. The pottery produced high quality earthenwares dubbed "opaque porcelain" and decorated largely in transfer printed patterns in colors other than blue, as was the trend during this period. Their wares ranged from dinner, dessert, tea, and breakfast services to toilet articles. Ornamentation varied from plain to decorative. The company's stoneware jugs were particularly well received.

Charles Meigh took his son, also Charles, into the business. After a brief stint as Charles Meigh, Son & Pankhurst in a brief partnership from 1849-1851, the name was changed to Charles Meigh & Son from 1851 to 1861. In 1861 Charles Meigh transferred the business to a limited liability company known as "The Old Hall Earthenware Company."

Charles Meigh built the pottery into a large establishment, as The Art Journal indicated, "The manufactory of Messrs. Charles Meigh & Sons ... is one of the largest and oldest in the pottery district ... in proof of its extent ... upward of 700 hands are employed there in the various departments; that more than 250 tons of coal are consumed every week; and that, during the same short space of time, 80 tons of clay are made into their various articles of manufacture." (The Art Journal Illustrated Catalogue 1851)

Above and right: **Susa** supper plate by Charles Meigh & Son. 9" in diameter. *Courtesy of L.B. Gaignault.* $60-65.

Series and Views — Charles Meigh & Son

Jenny Lind

Left and below: **Tivoli** egg platter by Charles Meigh. 9" x 6.5". *Courtesy of L.B. Gaignault.* $75-80.

Jenny Lind supper plate (early printing) by Charles Meigh & Son. 9" in diameter. *Courtesy of L.B. Gaignault.* $60-65.

Marks

Job Meigh used an impressed name mark "MEIGH" from 1805-1834, an impressed or printed "OLD HALL" mark in 1805 and the initials "J. M. & S." when his son Charles joined him in c. 1812. This mark was used, at times in conjunction with a printed design, until 1834.

From 1835 to 1849, Charles Meigh created many impressed marks featuring his full name. The majority of Charles Meigh's printed marks used the initials "C. M." with the pattern name and body type. Many marks included the Royal Arms.

When Charles Meigh's son Charles joined the firm in 1851 the initials on the variety of printed marks employed were changed to "C. M. & S." or "M. & S." This would continue until 1861. Pattern names and body types were frequently included. The Royal Arms were incorporated into several marks.

John Meir & Son

John Meir produced printed earthenwares at the Greengates Pottery of Tunstall, from c. 1812 to 1836. John Meir's son joined the firm in 1837 and the pottery continued on as John Meir & Son from 1837 to 1897.

Series and Views

Italian Scenery

A series of Italian views surrounded by floral borders with small landscape medallions. Seventeen different scenes have been recoreded, all printed in light blue.

Roselle

This pattern was registered by John Meir & Son in August 1848. (Coysh & Henrywood 1982, 309)

Roselle waste bowl by John Meir & Son. 6.5" in diameter. *Courtesy of L.B. Gaignault.* $75-80.

Marks

The early John Meir marks were impressed "MEIR" marks. Later, the firm switched to "J.M." or "I.M." printed marks. Beginning in 1837, John Meir & Son used the initials "J.M. & S."

Mellor, Venerables & Company

Mellor, Venables & Company produced earthenwares and china from the Hole House Pottery, Burslem, Staffordshire from 1834 to 1851. The company produced a variety of transfer printed earthenwares for the American market. The company also produced romantic views including Burmese, Medici, and Ning Po.

Far left and left: **Italian Scenery** supper plate by John Meir. 9" in diameter. *Courtesy of L.B. Gaignault.* $50-55.

Series and Views

Burmese

Above and right: **Burmese** dinner soup plate by Mellor, Venables & Company. 10.5" in diameter. *Courtesy of L.B. Gaignault.* $130-140.

Medici

Medici pie plate by Mellor, Venables & Company. *Courtesy of L.B. Gaignault.* $30-35.

Ning Po

Ning Po supper plate by Mellor, Venables & Company. 9.25" in diameter. *Courtesy of L.B. Gaignault.* $40-45.

Marks

The name, either printed out or as the initials "M. V. & CO.", is the standard feature of several impressed or printed marks. The printed pattern name is also frequently included.

David Methven & Sons

David Methven established himself at Kirkcaldy Pottery in Fife, Scotland producing earthenwares c. 1840. David Methven died in 1861 and the pottery was taken over by Andrew R. Young, who retained the David Methven & Sons name. Various members of the Young family continued to produce pottery under this name until 1930.

Series and Views

Palestine

Palestine platter by David Methven & Sons. 18" x 14.5" *Courtesy of James & Elizabeth Dunn, Bittersweet Antiques.* $340-375.

Marks

The early wares were usually unmarked. The initials "D.M. & S" or the full name of the firm appear regularly on wares dating from c. 1875 onward.

David Methven & Sons, Kirkcaldy Pottery, Fife, Scotland, c. 1840-1930. "D.M. & S." mark, or the full name, was used on later wars. David Methven died in 1861 and the pottery was taken over by Andrew R. Young, who retained the David Methven & Sons name.

Minton

"Of the variety of productions of Minton's works in former and present times it is impossible to speak in detail. So varied, so distinct, and so extensive are they in material, in body, in style, in decoration, and in uses, that anything like a detailed account becomes impossible." — Llewellynn Jewitt, 1877.

The venerable Minton firm produced earthenwares, porcelains, parian wares, majolica, and more under various titles (Minton, Minton & Boyle -c. 1836-41, Minton & Co. - c. 1841-73, Minton & Hollins - c. 1845-68) in Stoke from their establishment in 1793 on into the present day.

Founded at Stoke-on-Trent by Thomas Minton in 1793, the Minton factory has a tradition of producing high quality and widely varied ceramics which continues today. Thomas' son Herbert took over the works in 1836 and maintained control until 1858, greatly expanding and modernizing the factory and its range of wares during his tenure.

Among Thomas Minton's early contributions were tablewares in blue transfer printed cream-colored earthenwares. The firm's tablewares were produced in semi-porcelain bodies as well as ironstone china, white eathenware, and bone china. Transfer prints included Oriental, Renaissance and Gothic patterns which were designed in the early nineteenth century and continued to be used throughout the century. Under Herbert Minton, the factory kept tablewares as their mainstay but branched out into other areas as well, producing fine porcelain, parian figures, majolica, porcelains decorated by foreign artists in the Sèvres-style, and Pâte-sur-Pâte vases. To insure high quality wares, Minton's employed the most skilled artisans. Herbert Minton saw that the firm competed, and won high honors regularly, at the international exhibitions, beginning with the Great Exhibition of 1851 where he introduced majolica.

One of the effects of Herbert Mintons' modernization of the plant was to lower his cost of producing the formerly expensive table services without cheapening the appearance. Herbert Minton also produced blue transfer printed wares with improved technique and quality at a time when the quality of many potters' transfer prints were in decline.

The Minton pottery's contribution to Romantic Staffordshire included the views Chinese Marine and Genevese.

Series and Views

Chinese Marine

A pattern series featuring stylized Chinese landscapes introduced by Minton and copied by other potters. The quality of the Minton patterns is superior to those of the other potters.

Chinese Marine footed dish by Thomas Minton. 12" x 9.5" x 5.5" high. *Courtesy of L.B. Gaignault.* $200-220. (Another view on opposite page, top left)

The inner view of photo on opposite page bottom right:

Genevese

Above and right: **Genevese** dinner soup plate by Minton. 10" in diameter. *Courtesy of L.B. Gaignault.* $120-130.

Marks

From 1793 to 1806, Thomas Minton was in partnership with Joseph Poulson, a ceramicist, and traded under the name Minton & Poulson. The firm then traded under the names Minton & Boyle until 1836, Herbert Minton & Company until 1841, Minton & Company until 1845, and Mintons Ltd. beginning in 1873.

A wide variety of impressed and printed marks were used incorporating the "MINTON" name. The impressed mark read as "MINTONS" beginning in 1873. The impressed initials "B.B." were used during the mid-nineteenth century to indicate Best Body. Year cyphers were also employed by the firm from 1842 on. These marks occur in threesomes featuring a month letter, potter's mark, and the year cypher.

Samuel Moore & Company

(Samuel) Moore & Company manufactured earthenware ceramics at the Wear Pottery, Southwick, Sunderland, Durham from 1803 to 1882. Throughout this period, the company produced blue printed earthenwares, among others, under this name despite several changes in management.

Series and Views

Oriental

Oriental open vegetable dish by Samuel Moore and Company. 10" x 8". *Courtesy of James & Elizabeth Dunn, Bittersweet Antiques.* $130-140.

Marks

Printed and impressed marks were used and included the initial mark "S.M. & Co."

Francis Morley & Company

Francis Morley & Company was producing earthenwares, ironstones and other white bodied earthenwares at Broad Street, Shelton, Hanley, Staffordshire from 1845 to 1858. The firm had previously been Ridgway & Morley and would become Morley & Ashworth. The firm acquired the equipment of Charles J. Mason & Company, their engraver, and the rights to use the Mason's Patent Ironstone China name and mark.

Series and Views

American Marine

This pattern name encompassed a number of patterns featuring sailing boats within a border with four medallions with additional marine views. This pattern was produced in blue over a long period and was continued by the firm's successor, G.L. Ashworth & Bros.

Lake

A series of views produced by Francis Morley, Morley & Ashworth, and G.L. Ashworth & Bros.

Lake supper plate by Francis Morley & Company. 9" in diameter. *Courtesy of L.B. Gaignault.* $75-80.

American Marine side plate by Francis Morley & Company. 7.25" in diameter. *Courtesy of L.B. Gaignault.* $70-75.

Lake supper plate and side plate by Francis Morley & Company. 9" diameter supper plate; 7.25" diameter side plate. *Courtesy of L.B. Gaignault.* Supper plate: $75-80; side plate: $50-55.

Vista

Above and right: **Vista** luncheon plate by Francis Morley & Company, Shelton. 8" in diameter. *Courtesy of L.B. Gaignault.* $35-40.

Marks

This firm produced a number of impressed and printed marks with the initials "F. M.", "F. M. & CO." or with the full name of the firm "F. MORLEY & CO."

Richard Newbold

Unidentified

An unidentified Eastern scene adorns this covered vegetable dish, the handles of which are in the forms of sea shells. The ladle is missing. The author W.L. Little believed this pattern may have been produced by Richard Newbold of Lane End (Little 1969). 9" high x 15" wide. *Courtesy of Dora Landey.*

J.W. Pankhurst & Company

J.W. Pankhurst & Company produced ironstone earthenware ceramics (among others) from 1850 to 1882 at Charles Street and Old Hall Street.

Series and Views

Lucerne

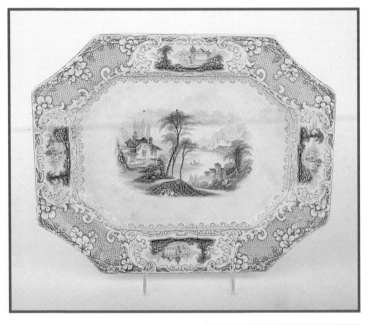

Above and right: **Lucerne** platter by J.W. Pankhurst & Company (the successor to W. Ridgway). 12.5" x 9.5". *Courtesy of L.B. Gaignault.* $175-190.

Marks

The words "& Co." were added to the Pankhurst printed marks around 1852.

George Phillips

George Phillips produced earthenwares in Longport from 1834 to 1848. Among his many blue printed patterns are "Canova", "Park Scenery", "Marine", and "Verona". A number of floral patterns were also produced.

Series and Views

Cambrian

Left and above: **Cambrian** dinner soup plate by George Phillips. 10.5" in diameter. *Courtesy of L.B. Gaignault.* $75-80.

Corinth

Corinth shallow potato bowl by George Phillips. 11" in diameter. *Courtesy of L.B. Gaignault.* $120-130.

Marino

Left and below: **Marino** large waste bowl by George Phillips. *Courtesy of L.B. Gaignault.* $60-65.

Ceylonese

Ceylonese supper plate by George Phillips. 9.5" in diameter. *Courtesy of L.B. Gaignault.* $50-55.

Park Scenery

A series of romantic scenes printed in blue and green.

Above and right: **Park Scenery** open vegetable dish by George Phillips. 10.5" x 9". *Courtesy of L.B. Gaignault.* $175-190.

Marks

George Phillips used a number of impressed and printed marks with either the name "Phillips" or "G. Phillips". These are frequently accompanied by the pattern name. The Staffordshire knot accompanied by the names "Phillips" and "Longport" was a mark also in use during this period.

Printed George Phillips "G. Phillips" manufacturer's mark in use from c. 1834 to 1848. *Courtesy of James & Elizabeth Dunn, Bittersweet Antiques.*

Podmore, Walker & Company

The company began their operations in Tunstall in 1834. The firm continued as Podmore, Walker & Company until 1859. Enoch Wedgwood became a partner in the pottery in c. 1856. Between c. 1856-1859, the firm used the mark "P.W. & W." for Podmore, Walker & Wedgwood. Enoch Wedgwood took over the older establishment in 1859 and changed the name to Wedgwood & Company.

The product of the firm was dinner and toilet sets in earthenware bodies heralded as Pearl Stone Ware and Imperial Ironstone China. The wares were brightly painted, sponged, or decorated with transfer prints.

Series and Views

Verona

Verona sugar bowl by George Phillips, c. 1835. 7" wide x 6" high. *Courtesy of James & Elizabeth Dunn, Bittersweet Antiques.* $100-110.

Juvenile

Below: **Juvenile** handleless cup by Podmore, Walker & Company. 4.25" in diameter. *Courtesy of L.B. Gaignault.* $50-55.

Olympia

Above and left: **Olympia** dinner plate by Podmore, Walker & Company. 10.5" in diameter. *Courtesy of L.B. Gaignault.* $125-135.

Venus

Above and right: **Venus** soup tureen base and egg platter by Podmore, Walker & Company. 9.5" diameter tureen; 10" x 7.5" platter. *Courtesy of L.B. Gaignault.* Tureen base: $90-100; platter: 75-80.

Spartan

Spartan chamber pot by Podmore, Walker & Company. 8.5" in diameter, 6" high. *Courtesy of L.B. Gaignault.* $175-190.

Marks

Podmore, Walker & Company used the initials "P.W. & CO." on several printed and impressed marks from 1834-1859 and frequently included the pattern names. The initials "P.W. & W." were employed from c. 1856-1859 when Enoch Wedgwood joined the firm.

Read & Clementson

This firm produced ironstone earthenwares at High Street, Shelton, Hanley, from 1833 to 1835.

Series and Views

Mantua

Above and right: **Mantua** dinner plate by Read & Clementson. 10.5" in diameter. *Courtesy of L.B. Gaignault.* $90-100.

Marks

Read & Clementson used several printed "R. & C." marks, frequently accompanied by pattern names.

Ridgway & Morley

Ridgway & Morley produced earthenwares at Broad Street, Shelton, Hanley, from 1842 to 1844. The company had been known previously as Ridgway, Morley, Wear & Company. Examples of both firms' patterns are shown in this book.

Series and Views

Nice

Pantheon

A series of romantic scenes, each of which includes temple ruins.

Pantheon platter by Ridgway & Morley. 13" x 9.5". *Courtesy of L.B. Gaignault.* $200-220.

Pheasant

Marks

This firm used printed manufacturer's marks using either the full name or the company's initials "R. & M."

Nice open vegetable dish and gray side plate by Ridgway & Morley. 9" x 11" open vegetable dish; 7" diameter side plate. *Courtesy of L.B. Gaignault.* Open vegetable dish: $150-165; side plate: $45-50.

The Ridgway Family

The Ridgway family were Staffordshire potters primarily associated with two Hanley potteries, the Bell Works (1792) and Cauldon Place (1802). Two brothers, Job and George Ridgway, formed a partnership until Job Ridgway built Cauldon Works. Job was joined by his sons John and William Ridgway from c. 1808 to 1814. The wares produced maintained a very high quality and the American views were well received. The Ridgway brothers enjoyed a thriving export business with America.

John and William ran the works from 1814 to 1830, producing dinner wares sold to the American export market among others. After 1830, until c. 1855, John directed the Cauldon Place Works while William ran the Bell Works. Cauldon Place Works would pass into the hands of Brown-Westhead, Moore & Company in 1862 and then to Cauldon Ltd. in 1905.

The Ridgway potteries produced useful wares of high workmanship in earthenwares, stonewares, and porcelain. Tea and dessert sets were specialties of the Ridgways. After 1830, William Ridgway manufactured finely molded jugs, stonewares, teapots, and candlesticks as well as delicate and finely decorated porcelain-styled tinted earthenware and stone china.

The Cauldon Place Works ceramics were described by Jewitt as, "... embrac[ing] almost every description of ceramic. In earthenware, all the usual table and toilet services and useful and ornamental articles of every class are made." (Jewitt 1877)

Tuscan Rose covered sauce tureen without ladle by John & William Ridgway, c. 1814-27. 6" high x 7.5" wide. *Courtesy of James & Elizabeth Dunn, Bittersweet Antiques.* $170-190.

Series and Views — John & William Ridgway

Tuscan Rose

Series and Views — John Ridgway & Company

Aladdin

Aladdin luncheon plate by John Ridgway, 1830-1855. 8" in diameter. *Courtesy of L.B. Gaignault.* $40-45.

Tuscan Rose supper plate by John & William Ridgway, c. 1825. 9" in diameter. *Courtesy of James & Elizabeth Dunn, Bittersweet Antiques.* $80-85.

Archipelago

A series of patterns featuring sailing boats with a floral border. These patterns were printed in blue and pink.

Above and left: **Archipelago** dinner plate by John Ridgway & Company. 10.25" in diameter. *Courtesy of L.B. Gaignault.* $90-100.

Above and right: **Archipelago** dinner plate by John Ridgway & Company. 10.25" in diameter. *Courtesy of L.B. Gaignault.* $90-100.

Beauties

Beauties supper plate by John Ridgway. 9.25" in diameter. *Courtesy of L.B. Gaignault.* $100-110.

Baronial Castles

Above and left: **Baronial Castles** platter by John Ridgway & Company. 17.25" x 14". *Courtesy of L.B. Gaignault.* $350-385.

Berlin Vase

Chinese

Above and right: **Berlin Vase** wash bowl by John Ridgway. 12.5" in diameter. *Courtesy of L.B. Gaignault.* $275-300.

Above and right: **Chinese** side plate by John Ridgway & Company. 7.25" in diameter. *Courtesy of L.B. Gaignault.* $40-45.

Delaware

This light blue romantic scene by John Ridgway does not represent any part of the American state.

Right: **Delaware** side plate by John Ridgway. 7" in diameter. *Courtesy of L.B. Gaignault.* $35-40.

Left: **Berlin Vase** luncheon plate by John Ridgway. 9.25" in diameter. *Courtesy of L.B. Gaignault.* $90-100.

Doria

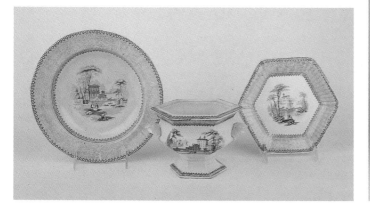

Doria hexagonal pie plate, luncheon soup plate, footed but lidless sugar bowl by John Ridgway. Soup plate: 9.25" in diameter; sugar bowl: 5.5" in diameter x 4.5" high. *Courtesy of L.B. Gaignault.* Pie plate: $50-55; luncheon soup plate: $65-70; sugar bowl: 75-80.

Giraffe teapot by J. Ridgway, c. 1835. 11" wide x 7" high. *Courtesy of James & Elizabeth Dunn, Bittersweet Antiques.* $545-600.

Giraffe

Giraffe teapot by John Ridgway, c. 1836. 7" high x 10". *Courtesy of Dora Landey.* $445-500.

Giraffe platter by John Ridgway, c. 1836. Printed on the back of the platter is the phrase, "Published Aug. 30th 1836 Agreeably to the Act" and "Stone Ware". 19.5" x 16.25" *Courtesy of Dora Landey.*

Far left and left: **Giraffe** dinner soup plate by John Ridgway, c. 1836. 10" in diameter. *Courtesy of James & Elizabeth Dunn, Bittersweet Antiques.* $215-235.

Giraffe handleless cup and saucer by John Ridgway. Saucer: 5.75" in diameter; cup: 4" wide. *Courtesy of James & Elizabeth Dunn, Bittersweet Antiques.* $140-155.

Japonica

Olympian

Japonica well and tree platter by John Ridgway, c. 1830-40. 21" x 16". *Courtesy of James & Elizabeth Dunn, Bittersweet Antiques.* $400-440.

Japonica waste bowl by John Ridgway, c. 1835-45. 6.5" wide x 3.5" high. *Courtesy of James & Elizabeth Dunn, Bittersweet Antiques.* $85-90.

Above and right: **Olympian** dinner plate by John Ridgway, c. 1842. 10" in diameter. *Courtesy of James & Elizabeth Dunn, Bittersweet Antiques.* $95-105.

Olympian dinner soup plate and tea cup and saucer by John Ridgway. *Courtesy of L.B. Gaignault.* Dinner soup plate: $100-110; cup and saucer: $75-80.

Pomerania

A romantic series of views, each with a different building as the center design. These patterns decorated dinner ware. These patterns were printed in blue, pink, purple, and sepia.

Pomerania plate by John Ridgway, c. 1830-55. 6.75" in diameter. *Courtesy of James & Elizabeth Dunn, Bittersweet Antiques.* $40-45.

Palestine

Palestine side plate by John Ridgway. 7.25" in diameter. *Courtesy of L.B. Gaignault.* $35-40.

Pomerania platter by John Ridgway, c. 1845. 19.5" x 16". *Courtesy of James & Elizabeth Dunn, Bittersweet Antiques.* $450-495.

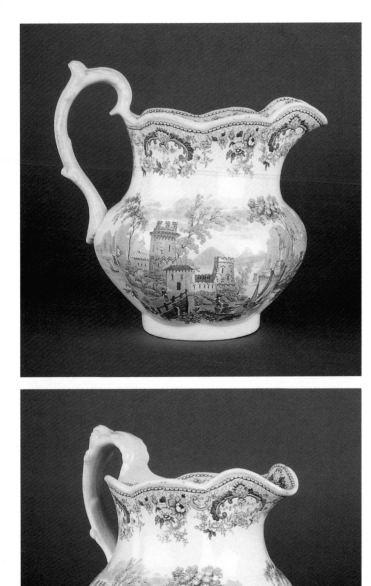

Royal Flora soup tureen without ladle by John Ridgway, c. 1835. 11.5" high x 13" wide. *Courtesy of James & Elizabeth Dunn, Bittersweet Antiques.* $625-685.

Seaweed

Above two: **Pomerania** pitcher by J. Ridgway, c. 1830. 6.25" high. *Courtesy of James & Elizabeth Dunn, Bittersweet Antiques.* $245-270.

Seaweed luncheon plate by John Ridgway, c. 1830-40. 8.25" in diameter. *Courtesy of James & Elizabeth Dunn, Bittersweet Antiques.* $45-50.

University luncheon plate by John Ridgway. 8.5" in diameter. *Courtesy of L.B. Gaignault.* $35-40.

Beauties II Falconry dinner plate by William Ridgway, c. 1830-41. 10.5" in diameter. *Courtesy of James & Elizabeth Dunn, Bittersweet Antiques.* $95-105.

Marks

John Ridgway, Cauldon Place, Shelton, Hanley, printed "J.R." manufacturer's mark in use from c. 1830 to 1841. *Courtesy of James & Elizabeth Dunn, Bittersweet Antiques.*

Series and Views— William Ridgway & Comany

Amoy

Right: **Amoy** footed vegetable dish by William Ridgway. 10" wide. *Courtesy of L.B. Gaignault.* $120-130.

Euphrates

Marmora

Above and right: **Euphrates** dinner plate by William Ridgway, 1834. 10.5" in diameter. *Courtesy of L.B. Gaignault.* $100-110.

Above and right: **Marmora** dinner plate by William Ridgway & Company. 10.25" in diameter. *Courtesy of L.B. Gaignault.* $80-85.

Grecian

Neva

Below: **Neva** soup tureen base by William Ridgway. Note the differences in scenes. 9.5" in diameter. *Courtesy of L.B. Gaignault.* $75-80.

Above and right: **Grecian** platter by William Ridgway. 17" x 14". *Courtesy of L.B. Gaignault.* $300-330.

Persian dinner plate by William Ridgway, c. 1830-34. 10.5" in diameter. *Courtesy of James & Elizabeth Dunn, Bittersweet Antiques.* $95-105.

Above two: **Oriental** pedestaled trifle bowl by William Ridgway. 10.5" in diameter. *Courtesy of L.B. Gaignault.* $300-330.

Osterley Park

Persian covered sugar bowl by William Ridgway, c. 1830. 8" wide x 6" high. *Courtesy of James & Elizabeth Dunn, Bittersweet Antiques.* $150-165.

Osterley Park sauce tureen missing its lid by Ridgway. This is a rare item. 7.5" handle to handle. *Courtesy of L.B. Gaignault.* $110-120.

149

Tyrolean

A series of Alpine views featuring mountains, people, and buildings.

Tyrolean platter by William Ridgway and Company, c. 1840. 12.75" x 10.25". *Courtesy of James & Elizabeth Dunn, Bittersweet Antiques.* $260-285.

Printed William Ridgway, Bell Works, Shelton, and Church Works, Hanley, "W.R." manufacturer's mark in use from c. 1830 to 1834. *Courtesy of James & Elizabeth Dunn, Bittersweet Antiques.*

Printed William Ridgway and Company "W.R. & Co." manufacturer's mark in use from 1834 to 1854. *Courtesy of James & Elizabeth Dunn, Bittersweet Antiques.*

Tyrolean water pitcher by William Ridgway, c. 1840. 7" high. *Courtesy of James & Elizabeth Dunn, Bittersweet Antiques.* $125-135.

Printed William Ridgway "W.R." manufacturer's mark in use from c. 1830 to 1834. *Courtesy of James & Elizabeth Dunn, Bittersweet Antiques.*

Tyrolean wash basin and pitcher by William Ridgway and Company, c. 1834-54. Pitcher: 10.5" high; wash basin: 13" wide x 4.75" high. *Courtesy of James & Elizabeth Dunn, Bittersweet Antiques.* $545-600.

A View of Venice
(See page 5)

Series and Views — William Ridgway, Son & Company

Forget-me-not

Rural Scenery

A series of country views. A series by this name was also produced by John & William Ridgway.

Above and right: **Rural Scenery** luncheon soup plate by William Ridgway, Son & Company. 9.25" in diameter. *Courtesy of L.B. Gaignault.* $75-80.

Above, left and below: **Forget-me-not** cup by William Ridgway & Company, 1834-1854. 3.75" in diameter. *Courtesy of M. R. Markowitz.* $25-30.

Union

Left and below: **Union** dinner plate by William Ridgway, Son & Company. 10.25" in diameter. *Courtesy of L.B. Gaignault.* $90-100.

Marks

The Ridgway family used a number of printed and impressed marks of varying designs. One regular feature was the presence of the family name or initials in the marks.

From 1814 to 1830 the name or initials of John & William Ridgway were used as "J. W. R.", "J. & W. R." or "J. & W. Ridgway". These were often included with the pattern name.

From c. 1830-1854, William Ridgway used his name "W. RIDGWAY" or initials with a variety of mark designs. In c. 1841 his son joined him and the name became "W. RIDGWAY, SON & CO." on the marks.

Ridgway, Morley, Wear & Company

This pottery produced earthenware ceramics from 1836 to 1842 at Broad Street, Shelton, Hanley. From 1842 to 1844, this firm was renamed Ridgway & Morley.

Series and Views

Agricultural Vase

This pattern with its prominent two-handled covered vase and river scenery was also produced by this company's successors Ridgway & Morley and Francis Morley & Company.

Above and right: **Japan Flowers** luncheon plate by Ridgway, Morley, Wear & Company, c. 1836-42, 8" in diameter. *Courtesy of James & Elizabeth Dunn, Bittersweet Antiques.* $45-50.

Above and left: **Agricultural Vase** dinner plate by Ridgway, Morley, Wear & Company. 10.25" in diameter. *Courtesy of L.B. Gaignault.* $50-55.

Japan Flowers plate by Ridgway, Morley, Wear & Company, and Company, c. 1836-42. 6.5" diameter. *Courtesy of James & Elizabeth Dunn, Bittersweet Antiques.* $35-40.

Japan Flowers wash basin and pitcher by Ridgway, Morley, Wear & Company, c. 1836-42. Pitcher: 10.5" high; bowl: 13" in diameter x 4.5" high. *Courtesy of James & Elizabeth Dunn, Bittersweet Antiques.* $425-465.

John & Richard Riley

This pottery produced both earthenwares and porcelains from Nile Street between c. 1802 and 1814 and Hill Works, Burslem, from c. 1814 to 1828. The Rileys' Hill Works pottery would later be handed over to Samuel Alcock.

Series and Views

"Girl Musician"

Above and right: **"Girl Musician"** vegetable dish by John & Richard Riley. 12" x 9". *Courtesy of L.B. Gaignault.* $100-110.

Marks

Ridgway, Morley, Wear & Company identified their wares with printed manufacturer's marks using either the firm's full name or the initials "R.M.W. & Co." throughout their period of production.

Ridgway, Morley, Wear & Company, Broad Street, Shelton, Hanley, 1836-42, printed "R.M.W. & Co." manufacturer's mark. *Courtesy of James & Elizabeth Dunn, Bittersweet Antiques.*

Ridgway, Morley, Wear & Company, Broad Street, Shelton, Hanley, printed "R.M.W. & Co." manufacturer's mark in use from 1836 to 1842. *Courtesy of James & Elizabeth Dunn, Bittersweet Antiques.*

153

An unidentified flowers in vase pattern platter by John & Richard Riley. 15" x 12". *Courtesy of Dora Landey.*

Marks

John & Richard Riley used a variety of painted, printed, impressed, and molded manufacturer's marks including "J. & R. Riley", "Riley's Semi China", and "RILEY".

John & Richard Riley, Nile Street, c. 1802-1814, and Hill Works, 1814-1828, Burslem, impressed "RILEY" manufacturer's mark.

Rockingham Works

Rockingham Works had a variety of owners from c. 1745 to 1842. This pottery works was located at Nr. Swinton, Yorkshire and produced both earthenwares and porcelains.

"Returning Woodman" bowl by Rockingham Works. 13.75" in diameter. *Courtesy of Dora Landey.*

Marks

Unlike what one might expect, this firm used a variety of impressed "BRAMELD" manufacturer's marks from 1806 to 1842.

Impressed partial "BRAMELD" manufacturer's mark for Rockingham Works, Nr. Swinton, Yorkshire, c. 1745-1842. This mark was in use from 1806 to 1842. *Courtesy of Dora Landey.*

John Rogers & Son

John Rogers and his son Spencer produced good quality earthenwares at Dale Hall, Longport, Staffordshire from c. 1814 to 1836 when the pottery closed. The firm produced large amounts of ceramics in a range of patterns and shapes. These were manufactured largely for the English market. Unlike most Staffordshire potters, Rogers & Son limited themselves to only a few special patterns for the American export market.

Series and Views

Fallow Deer soup tureen and underplate by John Rogers & Son. Tureen: 8.5" high x 13"; underplate: 16" x 10". *Courtesy of Dora Landey.*

English Views

English Views platter by John Rogers & Son, c. 1820. 13" x 10.5" *Courtesy of James & Elizabeth Dunn, Bittersweet Antiques.* $225-250.

"Roger's Zebra"

"Rogers' Zebra" wash basin by John Rogers & Son. 12" in diameter. *Courtesy of Dora Landey.*

Fallow Deer

Left and below: **Fallow Deer** sauce tureen with underplate and ladle by John Rogers & Son. Tureen: 5" high x 7.75"; underplate: 8.5" x 5". *Courtesy of Dora Landey.*

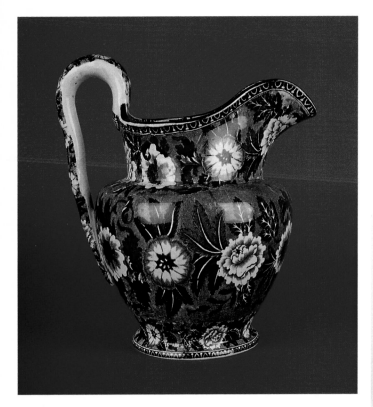

One of many unidentified views decorates this wash pitcher by John Rogers & Sons (Dale Hall, Longport, Burslem, 1815-1842). 10" high x 9". *Courtesy of Dora Landey.*

Marks

Rogers & Son used the impressed mark "ROGERS" which had previously been used by J. & G. Rogers. This mark was in use from c. 1784 to 1836. Geoffrey Godden states that many well potted blue printed wares bear this mark, most from the years 1800 to 1820. (Godden 1974)

John Rogers & Sons, Dale Hall, Longport, Burslem, 1815-1842, printed mark.

Anthony Shaw

Anthony Shaw produced earthenwares in the Staffordshire potting town of Tunstall from c. 1851 to 1856 and from Burslem from c. 1860 to 1900. His firm produced the romantic pattern Peruvian Horse Hunt. For the American export market, Shaw also produced a series of views from the 1846-1848 war with Mexico sparked by the breakdown of negotiations between the United States and Mexico over the purchase of New Mexico. American troops move into the disputed territory, defeating the Mexican troops at Palo Alto. The United States at that point declared war, moves into Santa Fe and annexed New Mexico. All of this occurred in five months from April of 1846 to August. In 1847, American forces captured Mexico city and in February of 1848 the Treaty of Guadalupe Hidalgo ended the war. The United States gained Texas, New Mexico, California, Utah, Nevada, Arizona, and portions of Colorado and Wyoming in the process.

Series and Views

Peruvian Horse Hunt

Peruvian Horse Hunt dinner plate, brown handleless cup, and a handleless cup and saucer by Anthony Shaw. The registration date is August 8, 1853. Dinner plate: 10.75" in diameter. *Courtesy of L.B. Gaignault.* Dinner plate: $125-135; brown handleless cup: $40-45; cup and saucer: $80-90.

Above and right: **Peruvian Horse Hunt** dinner plate, handleless cup and saucer by Anthony Shaw. The registration date is August 8, 1853. Dinner plate: 10.75" in diameter. *Courtesy of L.B. Gaignault.* Dinner plate: $125-135; cup and saucer: $80-90.

Texian Campaigne

Scenes from the war in this series, the total number of scenes is unclear, were printed in blue, purple, brown, red and black. These included:

the Battle of Buena Vista; the Battle of Monterey; the Battle of Palo Alto; the Battle of Resaca de la Palma; the Battle of Chapultepec; a General on a rearing horse, commanding his officers toward the distant battle; and Officers and men at rest around the fire.

C. & J. Shaw

This "Statue of Man on Horse" romantic pattern carries a "C. & J. Shaw backmark that is currently a mystery.

Series and Views

"Statue of Man on Horse"

Texian Campaigne supper plate by Anthony Shaw, c. 1851. 9.25" in diameter. *Courtesy of James & Elizabeth Dunn, Bittersweet Antiques.* $295-325.

Above and right: **"Statue of Man on Horse"** covered vegetable dish by C. & J. Shaw. 10.5" x 8.5". *Courtesy of L.B. Gaignault.* $90-100.

Marks

Shaw employed several impressed and printed marks. The common feature, the firm's name, appeared in its entirety, as "A. SHAW" or "SHAWS". Added to the mark was "& SON" from c. 1882 to c. 1898. This was altered to "& CO." from c. 1898 until the firm was purchased by A. J. Wilkinson Ltd. in about 1900.

Anthony Shaw, Tunstall, c. 1851-56, and Burslem, c. 1860 - c. 1900, printed pattern name and initials "J.B." which have been seen many times on this mark associated with the Shaw Texian Campaigne pattern. *Courtesy of James & Elizabeth Dunn, Bittersweet Antiques.*

Josiah Spode

Josiah Spode produced earthenwares, porcelains, and stone-chinas at Stoke-on-Trent from c. 1784 to April of 1833. The firm would then be renamed Copeland & Garrett.

Series and Views

Bridge of Lucano

Bridge of Lucano side plate by Josiah Spode. 6.75" in diameter. *Courtesy of L.B. Gaignault.* $75-80.

Convolvulus

A rare Spode floral pattern also known as Sunflower.

Convolvulus platter by Spode. 19 in by 14".
Courtesy of Dora Landey.

Marks

Josiah Spode employed a variety of painted, impressed, and printed manufacturer's marks including the printed "SPODE" mark on both earthenwares and porcelains after 1805 and a "Spode Stone China" mark from c. 1815 to 1830.

Andrew Stevenson

Andrew Stevenson produced vast supplies of dark blue printed earthenwares in Cobridge, Staffordshire between 1816 and 1830. Prior to 1816, Andrew Stevenson had been involved in the partnership of Bucknall and Stevenson.

Andrew Stevenson manufactured series of English views of country houses and castles. Many of these were exported to America, some with medallion portraits of George Washington and DeWitt Clinton. Most, however, sported borders of roses and other flowers.

Series and Views

"Pastoral Courtship"

"Pastoral Courtship" sauce tureen and underplate by Andrew Stevenson. Tureen: 4.5" high x 7"; underplate: 7" x 5". *Courtesy of Dora Landey.*

An unidentified rural scene with children decorates this wash basin by A. Stevenson. 5" high x 12.5" in diameter. *Courtesy of Dora Landey.*

Andrew Stevenson employed a variety of predominantly impressed marks. Difficulty in identification occurs when the name on the mark is simply "STEVENSON" as this could be attributable to either Andrew or his brother Ralph. Other impressed Andrew Stevenson marks include the name "A. STEVENSON" and "Stevenson" impressed in an arc over a three masted sailing ship.

Andrew Stevenson, Cobridge, impressed "A. Stevenson" circular manufacturer's mark in use from c. 1816 to 1830.

Andrew Stevenson, Cobridge, c. 1816-1830, impressed "Stevenson" manufacturer's mark with ship. One example of this mark bears the date 1820. (Godden 1974, 596)

An unidentified English rural scene on a wash basin with an impressed "A. Stevenson" mark. *Courtesy of Dora Landey.*

Ralph Stevenson / Ralph Stevenson & Williams

Ralph Stevenson began manufacturing well crafted and decorated earthenware on his own in Cobridge earlier than his brother Andrew. Ralph Stevenson produced his wares at the Lower Manufactory in Cobridge, Staffordshire from roughly 1810 to 1835. Around 1825, Ralph formed the short-lived partnership Ralph Stevenson & Williams. In 1832 Ralph was joined by his son. The pottery continued as Ralph Stevenson & Son until 1835.

Transfer printed wares decorated the majority of the earthenwares produced by Ralph Stevenson. Included among his Romantic Staffordshire series of views were British Lakes, British Palaces, Millenium, and Palestine.

Series and Views — Ralph Stevenson & Williams

Beehive and Vases

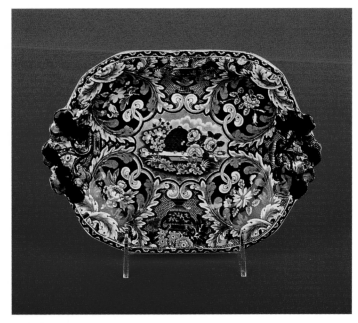

Beehive and Vases underplate by Stevenson and Williams, c. 1825. 8.75" x 6.5" *Courtesy of Dora Landey.*

Above and right: **Beehive and Vases** creamer by Stevenson and Williams, c. 1825. 4.25" high x 6.5" lip to handle. *Courtesy of Dora Landey.*

Marks

Stevenson & Williams, Lower Manufactory, Cobridge, printed "R.S.W." manufacturer's mark in use c. 1825.

Stevenson & Williams, Lower Manufactory, Cobridge, printed manufacturer's mark in use c. 1825.

Series and Views — Ralph Stevenson/Ralph Stevenson & Son

British Lakes

A series of British lake views from various waterways.

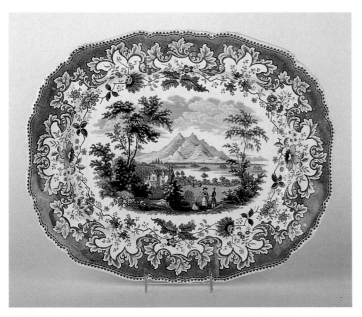

British Lakes platter by Ralph Stevenson & Son, c. 1832-35. 17" x 14". *Courtesy of James & Elizabeth Dunn, Bittersweet Antiques.* $350-385.

British Palaces covered sauce tureen with ladle and underplate by Ralph Stevenson, c. 1815. The covered sauce tureen measures 6" high; the ladle measures 6.5" long; the underplate measures 9" x 7.25". *Courtesy of James & Elizabeth Dunn, Bittersweet Antiques.* $475-525.

British Lakes plate by Ralph Stevenson & Son, c. 1832-35. *Courtesy of James & Elizabeth Dunn, Bittersweet Antiques.* NP

A second view of the British Palaces covered sauce tureen with ladle and underplate by Ralph Stevenson, c. 1815. Even the bowl of the ladle is decorated. *Courtesy of James & Elizabeth Dunn, Bittersweet Antiques.* $475-525.

Millennium

Above and right: **Millennium** platter by Ralph Stevenson. The words on platter read, "PEACE ON EARTH" "Give us this day our daily Bread"; the bible is open to Isaiah Ch. XI.VI. 17" x 13.75". *Courtesy of Dora Landey.*

Millennium luncheon plate by Ralph Stevenson & Son. 9" in diameter. *Courtesy of L.B. Gaignault.* $150-165.

Palestine

Palestine platter by Ralph Stevenson, c. 1810-32. 15.5" x 13". *Courtesy of Dora Landey.*

Millennium dinner plate by Ralph Stevenson and Company, c. 1832-35. 10.25" in diameter. *Courtesy of James & Elizabeth Dunn, Bittersweet Antiques.* $195-215.

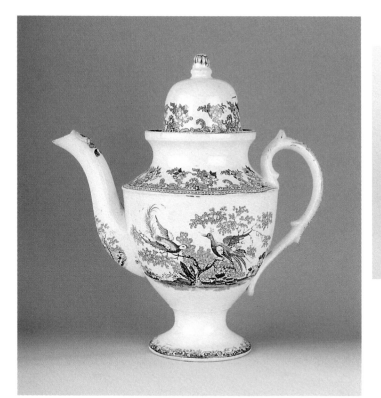

Above and bottom two: **"Semi-China Warranted"** series **Horseman at the Ford** pattern reticulated chestnut holder and undertray by Ralph Stevenson. 5" high x 10" wide. 10.75" x 8.5" undertray. *Courtesy of Dora Landey.*

Paroquet domed lid coffee pot by Stevenson, c. 1810-34. 11" high. *Courtesy of James & Elizabeth Dunn, Bittersweet Antiques.* $225-245.

"Semi-China Warranted" Series

A series of views including:
The Bull; Milkmaid and Goats; Boy and Dogs; Piping Shepherd Boy; The Three Donkeys; Horseman at the Ford; and Girl with Sheep and Goat.

"Semi-China Warranted" Series view known by the names **"Milkmaid & Goats"** or **"Man With a Rake."** by Ralph Stevenson, c. 1825. 10" in diameter. *Courtesy of Dora Landey.*

Unidentified

Marks

There is some confusion with these brothers' marks. Both had the nasty habit of simply using the "STEVENSON" name as their mark, making it difficult to deduce which Stevenson, Andrew or Ralph, actually produced the ware. Ralph Stevenson did use an impressed "R. STEVENSON" mark or his initials as well. He also used an arced "STEVENSON" mark over a crown with "STAFFORDSHIRE" printed in another arc below.

From c. 1832 to 1835 the mark changed to "R. STEVENSON & SON" or "R. S. & S." In c. 1825 several printed marks used the name or initials of a short-lived partnership "R. STEVENSON & WILLIAMS" or "R. S. W."

Ralph Stevenson & Son, Lower Manufactory, Cobridge, printed "R.S. & S." manufacturer's mark in use from c. 1832 to 1835.

Above, left and right: An unidentified flower and vase pattern on a large milk pitcher marked "Stevenson's Stone China" on the base. 9" high, 10" wide. *Courtesy of Dora Landey.*

164

Joseph Stubbs/Stubbs & Kent

Series and Views — Stubbs & Kent

Joseph Stubbs produced earthenwares at Dale Hall, Longport, Burslem, Staffordshire from c. 1822-1835. Stubbs printed his wares in dark blue, a color popular early in the American export market. Briefly, from 1828 to 1830, Joseph Stubbs worked in partnership as Stubbs & Kent.

Fruit and Flowers

Fruit and Flowers platter by Stubbs and Kent, Longport. 18.5" x 15.25". *Courtesy of Dora Landey.*

Series and Views — Joseph Stubbs

Unidentified

An unidentified sea shells pattern on a dinner plate by Joseph Stubbs, Longport. 10.25" in diameter. *Courtesy of Dora Landey.*

Woodman

Woodman covered sugar bowl by Joseph Stubbs (also produced by Spode). 4.5" high. *Courtesy of L.B. Gaignault.* $250-275.

Unidentified

An unidentified sea shells pattern on a well and tree platter by Stubbs and Kent Longport. Joseph Stubbs and Stubbs & Kent are both known for the habit of not naming their patterns. Sea shell patterns without names would continue to be produced by Joseph Stubbs from c. 1822 to 1835. 18.5" x 15.25" *Courtesy of Dora Landey.*

Marks

During the years of production from c. 1822-1835 Joseph Stubbs used impressed marks reading either simply "STUBBS" or "JOSEPH STUBBS LONGPORT". The second was printed in a circular form. From c. 1828 to 1830, the circular impressed mark "STUBBS & KENT LONGPORT" was used.

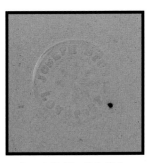

Joseph Stubbs, Dale Hall, Longport, Burslem, impressed "Joseph Stubbs Longport" circular manufacturer's mark in use from c. 1822-1835.

Stubbs & Kent, Dale Hall, Longport, Burslem, impressed circular manufacturer's mark in use from c. 1820 to 1830. *Courtesy of Dora Landey.*

Stubbs & Kent, Dale Hall, Longport, Burslem, impressed circular manufacturer's mark in use from c. 1820 to 1830. *Courtesy of Dora Landey.*

John Swift

John Swift produced printed earthenwares at Stafford and Flint Streets, Longton in c. 1843. Swiss Scenery was among his romantic patterns.

Series and Views

Swiss Scenery

Swiss Scenery bowl by John Swift, c. 1843. 5.75" in diameter. *Courtesy of James & Elizabeth Dunn, Bittersweet Antiques.* $30-35.

Swiss Scenery covered sauce tureen with underplate by John Swift, c. 1843. 8" wide x 6" high Underplate: 8.5" x 6.5" *Courtesy of James & Elizabeth Dunn, Bittersweet Antiques.* NP.

Marks

John Swift employed a printed "J.S." manufacturer's mark in c. 1843.

Printed "J.S." manufacturer's mark of John Swift, c. 1843.

E. T. Troutbeck

E. T. Troutbeck produced romantic Chinese Gem and Epirus patterns at Sandyford, Tunstall, in about 1846.

Series and Views

Epirus

Above, left and right: **Epirus** dinner plate by E. T. Troutbeck. 10.5" in diameter. *Courtesy of L.B. Gaignault.* $75-80.

Marks

Both printed and impressed full name marks were used by this pottery c. 1846.

Thomas Walker

Thomas Walker ran the Lion Works in Tunstall from 1845 to 1851. The firm produced a variety of blue printed earthenwares.

Series and Views

Kan-Su

650-651

Above and left: **Kan-Su** side plate by Thomas Walker. 7.75" in diameter. *Courtesy of L.B. Gaignault.* $35-40.

Tavoy side plate by Thomas Walker. 7.5" in diameter. *Courtesy of L.B. Gaignault.* $30-35.

Marks

Printed marks used by the pottery throughout their limited years of production include "T. WALKER" and "THOS WALKER".

The Wedgwood Potters

"The aim of the firm is, and always has been, to produce the best, most artistic, and most pleasingly effective designs, and to adapt them to ordinary purposes, so that they may become the everyday surroundings of the artisan as well as of the educated man of taste." — Llewellynn Jewitt, 1877.

Josiah Wedgwood I (1730-1795) established the pottery in Burslem in 1759 and it was controlled by the family until becoming a public company in 1967. Briefly, Josiah Wedgwood I's son, Josiah Wedgwood II was succeeded at the time of his death in 1841 by his sons Josiah III and Francis. Josiah III became a partner in 1823 and remained so until his retirement in 1842. Francis joined the firm as a partner in 1827 and controlled the company from 1842 to 1870. Francis went into a brief partnership with J. Boyle and Robert Brown. He took his sons Godfrey, Clement, Francis, and Lawrence into partnership between 1859 and 1865.

Wedgwood & Company produced a wide variety of fine earthenwares, stone chinas, and other wares from 1860 onward. This well-known pottery was located in Tunstall at the Unicorn Pottery, Amicable Street, and Pinnox Works. Podmore, Walker & Company used the Podmore, Walker & Wedgwood name from 1856 to 1859, making full use of the Wedgwood name. In 1860 this firm became Wedgwood & Company. Many of the earlier blue printed designs were continued by this company. The most famous pattern associated with this firm is Asiatic Pheasants.

Of the earthenware produced by Wedgwood, Jewitt reports, "The goods produced are higher classes of earthenware, in which dinner, tea, breakfast, dessert, toilet and other services, and all the usual miscellaneous articles, are made to a very considerable extent, both for the home, colonial, Continental, and American markets, to which considerable quantities are regularly exported." The company's "Imperial Ironstone China" was considered to be the staple of the firm. The quality was considered to be excellent and the decoration admirable. When exhibited at international exhibitions, Wedgwood ceramics received positive attention.

By the middle of the nineteenth century, when Wedgwood & Company was in operation, tablewares were mainly transfer printed. A variety of all covering patterns were based on chinoiserie views, floral studies, and other designs popular during the period.

Wedgwood's "Best patterns" were influenced by Oriental styles and were decorated with prunus blossoms, insects, bamboo leaves, birds, and angular patterns around the rim. These were initially flowing patterns. They may have first been offered at high prices too, if the firm followed the philosophy of its founder Josiah Wedgwood. Josiah Wedgwood I believed that quality goods must first be offered at high prices "...to make the[m] esteemed 'Ornaments for Palaces'..."

Series and Views — Wedgwood & Company

Eagle

Above and rigth: **Eagle** saucer by Wedgwood & Company. 6" in diameter. *Courtesy of L.B. Gaignault.* $30-35.

168

An unidentified rural pattern featuring a fisherman with his net. This pattern adorns a possible coffee cann by Wedgwood, c. 1830. 2.75" high by 3" wide. *Courtesy of James & Elizabeth Dunn, Bittersweet Antiques.* $75-80.

Marks

The Wedgwood custom was to meticulously mark their wares; these were Wedgwood products and they wanted their customers to know it. Nearly all their ceramics bear the impressed "WEDGWOOD" mark. "ENGLAND" was added in 1892 and "MADE IN ENGLAND" in 1911. Pattern names frequently appear. Various impressed and printed marks in a wide range of designs have been used over the years with the Wedgwood name, changing with time and association between several potting factories the family maintained.

Wedgwood also employed a three letter code in which the third letter represented the year, beginning in 1860.

Wedgwood & Company used printed and impressed marks from the start that featured the name "WEDGWOOD & CO.", often with the name of the earthenware body "Imperial Iron Stone China" included.

Wood & Challinor

Wood & Challinor produced earthenware ceramics in Tunstall at the Brownhills Pottery from 1828 to 1841 and at the Woodland Pottery from 1834 to 1843.

Chinese Temples

Above and right: **Chinese Temples** dinner plate by Wood & Challinor, 1828-1843. 10.25" in diameter. *Courtesy of L.B. Gaignault.* $110-120.

169

Corsica

Corsica supper plate by Wood & Challinor, c. 1828-43. 9.5" in diameter. *Courtesy of James & Elizabeth Dunn, Bittersweet Antiques.* $75-80.

Mesina

Above and right: **Mesina** supper plate by Wood & Challinor. 9.5" in diameter. *Courtesy of L.B. Gaignault.* $60-65.

Rimini

Left and below: **Rimini** dinner plate by Wood & Challinor. 10.25" in diameter. *Courtesy of L.B. Gaignault.* $80-85.

Marks

The initials "W. & C." identify this firm in a number of different marks, many of which included pattern names.

Wood & Challinor, Brownhills Pottery, 1828-41, Woodland Pottery, 1834-43, printed "W. & C." manufacturer's mark in use from 1828 to 1843. *Courtesy of James & Elizabeth Dunn, Bittersweet Antiques.*

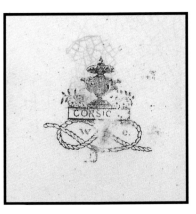

Enoch Wood & Sons

The Wood family produced nearly as many potters as the Adams family, thankfully not as unimaginatively named as the series of Williams. Of the Woods, Enoch Wood did very well with finely crafted transfer printed wares. Enoch Wood produced over eighty English views, a series of French views, and approximately fifty-eight American views.

Enoch Wood & Sons produced their quality transfer printed earthenwares out of Burslem from 1818 to 1846. Over time, Enoch Wood & Sons produced transfer prints that followed the popular trends of the day. Later prints were produced in colors other than blue and featuring romantic scenes in more open designs.

The most significant and appreciated of Enoch Wood & Son's output were the various series of views the firm produced. Each piece in a dinner service was decorated with a different view. A number of single view or pattern services were also produced.

Series and Views

Belzoni

A series of hunting scenes were produced under this title to decorate dinner and tea services. Most of the patterns feature hunters on horseback carrying bows and pennants.

Above and right: **Belzoni** platter by Enoch Wood & Sons. 15.5" x 13.5" in diameter. *Courtesy of L.B. Gaignault.* $300-330.

Above and right: **Belzoni** platter by Enoch Wood & Sons, c. 1818-46. 15" x 13". *Courtesy of James & Elizabeth Dunn, Bittersweet Antiques.* $400-440.

Belzoni dinner plate and waste bowl by Enoch Wood & Sons. Plate: 10.5" in diameter; waste bowl: 5.5" in diameter. *Courtesy of L.B. Gaignault.* Dinner plate: $95-105; waste bowl: $75-80.

Belzoni covered vegetable dish by Enoch Wood and Sons, c. 1830. 12" wide x 7" high. *Courtesy of James & Elizabeth Dunn, Bittersweet Antiques.* $375-415.

A series of designs including:
The Bride; Cupid Imprisoned; Cupid's Escape; Girl Behind Grape Fence; The Young Philosopher.

Cupid Imprisoned dinner plate by Enoch Wood & Sons, Burslem Warranted, part of the Cupid Series. 10" in diameter. *Courtesy of Dora Landey.*

Belzoni multi-colored pattern covered sugar bowl by Enoch Wood and Son, c. 1820. This is a very rare piece. 6" high by 8" wide. *Courtesy of James & Elizabeth Dunn, Bittersweet Antiques.* $260-285.

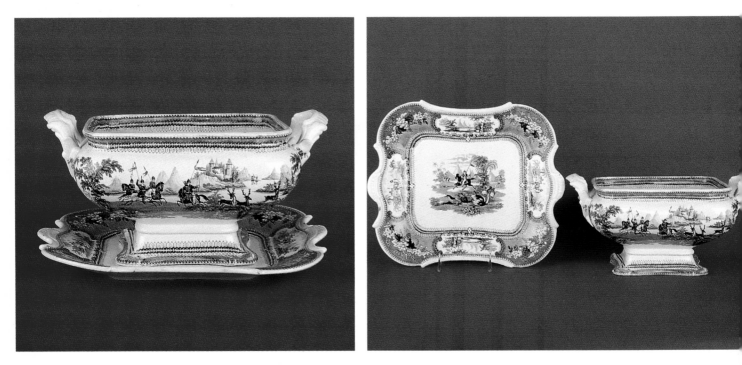

Belzoni soup tureen and undertray by Enoch Wood and Sons, c. 1825. Tureen: 14" wide x 8" x 6.5" high; undertray: 14.25" wide x 10.5". *Courtesy of James & Elizabeth Dunn, Bittersweet Antiques.* NP.

"**Girl Behind Grape Fence**" dinner soup plate, part of Cupid Series by Enoch Wood & Sons. 10" in diameter. *Courtesy of Dora Landey.*

A rare multi-colored **Festoon Border** supper plate by Enoch Wood & Sons, c. 1825. 9.25" in diameter. *Courtesy of James & Elizabeth Dunn, Bittersweet Antiques.* $125-135.

Fisherman

The Young Philosopher dinner plate by Enoch Wood & Sons, part of the Cupid Series. 10" in diameter. *Courtesy of Dora Landey.*

Center right and right: **Fisherman** luncheon plate by Enoch Wood & Sons, c. 1818-46. 8.25" in diameter. *Courtesy of James & Elizabeth Dunn, Bittersweet Antiques.* $95-105.

Fountain

Fountain cup plate by Enoch Wood & Sons. 4" in diameter. *Courtesy of James & Elizabeth Dunn, Bittersweet Antiques.* $60-65.

Grecian Scenery

Above and right: **Grecian Scenery** dinner soup plate by Enoch Wood & Sons. "Celtic China" is Wood & Sons' name for their ceramic ironstone body. 10.25" in diameter. *Courtesy of L.B. Gaignault.* $95-105.

London Views Series

A series of London city views including: Hanover Lodge, Regent's Park; Richmond Terrace, Whitehall; St. George's Chapel, Regent Street.

London Views Series platter featuring the **St. George's Chapel, Regent Street** pattern by Enoch Wood & Sons. 16" x 13". *Courtesy of Dora Landey.*

London Views Series, **Richmond Terrace, Whitehall** tureen by Enoch Wood & Sons. 7" high x 15". *Courtesy of Dora Landey.*

No. 107

No. 107 dinner plate by Enoch Wood & Sons. This is a rare multi-colored piece. 10.5" in diameter. *Courtesy of James & Elizabeth Dunn, Bittersweet Antiques.* NP.

Pekin

A rare multi-colored **Railway** supper plate by Enoch Wood & Sons. 9.25" in diameter. *Courtesy of James & Elizabeth Dunn, Bittersweet Antiques.* $150-165.

Pekin potato bowl, handleless cup and saucer, and a sugar bowl missing its lid by Enoch Wood. *Courtesy of L.B. Gaignault.* Potato bowl: $200-220; cup and saucer: $60-65; sugar bowl: $75-80.

Sporting Series

This series of sporting views was taken from Bewick's *A General History of Quadrupeds* and includes:
antelope; a pied goat; common antelope; gnu; grysbok; and tiger hunt.

Unidentified

Sporting Series **Tiger Hunt** well and tree platter by Enoch Wood & Sons. 18.75" x 14.5". *Courtesy of Dora Landey.*

An unidentified pattern dinner plate by Enoch Wood & Sons. 10" in diameter. *Courtesy of Dora Landey.*

Sporting Series **Antelope** saucer by Enoch Wood & Sons. 6.5" in diameter. *Courtesy of Dora Landey.*

An unidentified Oriental pattern featuring people and a peacock dinner plate by Enoch Wood & Sons. 10.5" in diameter. *Courtesy of Dora Landey.*

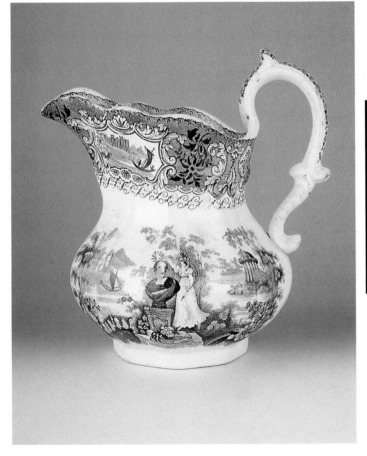

Venetian Scenery covered sugar bowl with a floral finial by Enoch Wood, c. 1818-46. 6.25" high x 8" wide. *Courtesy of James & Elizabeth Dunn, Bittersweet Antiques.* $115-125.

Washington pitcher by Enoch Wood and Sons, c. 1830. 8" high. *Courtesy of James & Elizabeth Dunn, Bittersweet Antiques.* $200-220.

Enoch Wood & Sons used a variety of impressed marks featuring the full name or the initials of the firm. The location of the pottery was also used either as "BURSLEM" or "BURSLEM STAFFORDSHIRE". The mark "E. & E. WOOD" was used briefly in c. 1840 and referred to Enoch and Edward Wood.

Enoch Wood & Sons, Fountain Place, Burslem, 1818-46, printed "E.W. & S." manufacturer's mark used throughout this period. *Courtesy of James & Elizabeth Dunn, Bittersweet Antiques.*

This E. Wood & Sons printed manufacturer's mark was in use from 1818 to 1846. *Courtesy of James & Elizabeth Dunn, Bittersweet Antiques.*

Enoch Wood & Sons, Fountain Place (among others), Burslem, "E.W. & S." printed manufacturer's mark in use from c. 1818 to 1846. *Courtesy of James & Elizabeth Dunn, Bittersweet Antiques.*

Enoch Wood & Sons, Fountain Place, Burslem, impressed "Semi China" circular mark with an eagle in the center manufacturer's mark in use from 1818 to 1846. These marks were often used on finely printed blue wares made for export to the American market. (Godden 1974, 686)

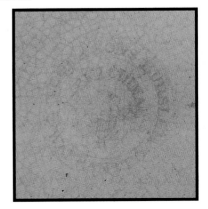

177

John Wedg Wood

John Wedg Wood took full advantage of the similarity between his name and that of Josiah Wedgwood. John Wedg Wood produced earthenwares at Burslem from 1841 to 1844 and Tunstall from 1845 to 1860.

Series and Views

Brussels

Columbia

Romantic scenes under this name were registered on August 23, 1848. (Coysh & Henrywood 1982, 90)

Columbia waste bowl by John Wedg Wood. 4.5" in diameter. *Courtesy of L.B. Gaignault.* $50-55.

Above and right: **Brussels** handleless cup and saucer by John Wedg Wood, c. 1841-60. Cup: 4" wide x 2.75" high; saucer: 6" in diameter. *Courtesy of James & Elizabeth Dunn, Bittersweet Antiques.* $65-70 cup and saucer set.

Festoon

Festoon saucer by John Wedg Wood. 6" in diameter. *Courtesy of L.B. Gaignault.* $35-40.

Seine

Seine supper plate by John Wedg Wood. 9.25" in diameter. *Courtesy of L.B. Gaignault.* $75-80.

Marks

Mr. Wedg Wood used several different printed marks, all of which displayed his name as "J. WEDGWOOD". Many have mistaken this for the mark of Josiah Wedgwood although Mr. Wedgwood never included the initial "J." in his marks. John Wedg Wood also used an impressed "W. W." mark.

John Wedg Wood, Burslem, 1841-44, Tunstall, 1845-60, "J. Wedgwood" printed manufacturer's mark in use from c. 1841 to 1860.

George Wooliscroft

The mobile George Wooliscroft produced earthenwares at Well Street in c. 1851, at High Street in c. 1853, and at the Sandyford Potteries (all in Tunstall) from c. 1860 to 1864.

Series and Views

Eon

A series of romantic-style patterns featuring a rural landscape with windmills. The patterns were registered on February 10, 1853. (Coysh & Henrywood 1989, 77)

Marks

This potter used his name "G. WOOLISCROFT", the ware type "Ironstone", and the pattern name in his impressed and printed marks.

Eon covered sugar bowl by G. Wooliscroft. 7.5" high. *Courtesy of L.B. Gaignault.* $150-165.

Recommended Reading

Arman, David & Linda. *Historical Staffordshire. An Illustrated Check-List.* Danville, Virginia: Arman Enterprises, Inc., 1974.

The Art Journal Illustrated Catalogue. *The Industry of All Nations 1851.* London: George Virtue, 1851.

Cameron, Elisabeth. *Encyclopedia of Pottery & Porcelain. 1800-1960.* New York: Facts on File Publications, 1986.

Carter, Tina M. *Teapots. The Collector's Guide to Selecting, Identifying, and Displaying New and Vintage Teapots.* Philadelphia, Pennsylvania: Running Press, 1995.

Copeland, Robert. *Spode's Willow Pattern and Other Designs after the Chinese.* New York: Rizzoli International Publications in association with Christie's, 1980.

Coysh, A. W. *Blue and White Transfer Ware, 1780-1840.* London & Vancouver: David & Charles, 1970.

Coysh, A. W. & R. K. Henrywood. *The Dictionary of Blue and White Printed Pottery. 1780-1880.* Volumes I & II. Woodbridge, Suffolk: Antique Collectors' Club, 1982 & 1989.

Dean, Patricia. *The Official Identification Guide to Pottery & Porcelain.* Orlando, Florida: The House of Collectibles, Inc., 1984.

Godden, Geoffrey A. *Encyclopaedia of British Pottery and Porcelain Marks.* New York: Bonanza Books, 1964.

_____, *The Concise Guide to British Pottery and Porcelain.* London: Barrie & Jenkins, 1990.

Halsey, R. T. Haines. *Pictures of Early New York on Dark Blue Staffordshire Pottery.* New York: Dover Publications, Inc., 1899.

Hughes, Bernard & Therle. *The Collector's Encyclopaedia of English Ceramics.* London: Abbey Library, 1968.

Jewitt, Llewellynn. *The Ceramic Art of Great Britain.* Poole, Dorset, England: New Orchard Editions Ltd., 1985. [reprint of 1877 original]

Laidacker, Sam. *Anglo-American China, Part I.* Bristol, Pennsylvania: Sam Laidacker, 1954. Second Edition.

Little, W. L. *Staffordshire Blue. Underglaze Blue Transfer-printed Earthenware.* New York: Crown Publishers, Inc., 1969.

Lockett, T. A. & P. A. Halfpenny (ed.). *Creamware & Pearlware. The Fifth Exhibition from the Northern Ceramic Society.* Stoke-on-Trent: George Street Press Ltd., 1986.

Noël Hume, Ivor. *All the Best Rubbish.* New York: Harper & Row, Publishers, 1974.

_____, *A Guide to Artifacts of Colonial America.* New York: Alfred A. Knopf, 1985.

Panati, Charles. *Panati's Extraordinary Endings of Practically Everything and Everybody.* New York: Harper & Row, Publishers, 1989.

Pratt, James Norwood. *Tea Lover's Treasury.* Santa Rosa, California: Cole Group, Inc., 1982.

Royal Commission. *Reports by the Juries on the Subject in the Thirty Classes into Which the Exhibition was Divided.* Volume III. London: W. Clowes & Sons, Printers, 1852.

Snyder, Jeffrey B. *Historical Staffordshire.* Atglen, Pennsylvania: Schiffer Publishing, Ltd., 1995.

_____. *Historic Flow Blue.* Atglen, Pennsylvania: Schiffer Publishing Ltd., 1994.

Tippett, Paul. *Christie's Collectibles. Teapots. The Connoisseur's Guide.* Boston, Massachusetts: Little, Brown and Company, 1996.

Williams, Petra. *Staffordshire. Romantic Transfer Patterns.* Jeffersontown, Kentucky: Fountain House East, 1978.

_____. *Staffordshire II. Romantic Transfer Patterns.* Jeffersontown, Kentucky: Fountain House East, 1986.

Index

Appendix

List of Pattern Series Produced on Blue-And-White Transfer-Printed Earthenware

This list has been compiled from the records of the Friends of Blue in England. The list presents only recorded items and is not to be considered complete or comprehensive. The names of each manufacturer is provided including former and subsequent names, partnerships, and so on where continuity is certain. In some cases patterns were produced by only one or more of the partnerships concerned, but frequently designs were used over the whole life of the factory, subject of course to prevailing fashion and demand.

Alternative series names, as a rule, have not been provided. For example, there are series that are known by different names in England and in the United States. Also, none of the Rowland and Marsellus patterns have been included as these are unrecorded in England.

British Views

Manufacturers	Pattern Series
ADAMS	Flowers and Leaves Border
	Regents Park
	Foliage and Scroll Border
	Bluebell Border
	Rocks and Foliage border
	Scottish Scenes
	Caledonia
BATHWELL & GOODFELLOW	Rural Scenery
J. D. BAGSTER	Vignette
	Metropolitan Scenery
BELLE VUE POTTERY	Belle Vue Views
BO'NESS POTTERY (Jamieson)	Modern Athens (Edinburgh Views)
CHARLES BOURNE	British Views
T. & J. CAREY	Cathdrals
	Irish Views
	Titled Seats
J. & R. CLEWS	Bluebell Border
	Select Scenery
	Foliage and Scroll Border
COPELAND AND GARRETT	Arabesque
DAVENPORT	Rustic Scenes
	Rural Scenery
	Mare and Foal
	Fishermen (Gothic Ruins)
	Muleteer
	Cornucopia Flower Border
ELKIN KNIGHT	Rock Cartouche
	Irish Scenery
	Baronial Halls
J. GOODWIN (Seacombe)	Views of London
GOODWIN AND HARRIS	Metropolitan Scenery
GRIFFITHS BEARDMORE & BIRKS	
R. HALL	Light Blue Rose Border
	Select Views
	Picturesque Scenery
CHARLES HARVEY	Towns and Cities

HENSHALL	Fruit and Flower Border
HERCULANEUM	Cherub Medallion Border
	Liverpool Views
JOHNSON BROS.	Old British Castles
S. KEELING	Baronial Views
R. A/ KIDSTON	United Kingdom
C. J. MASON	British Lakes
	College Views
T. MAYER	Cattle and Scenery
T. J. & J. MAYER	Baronial Halls
	Garden Scenery
C. MEIGH	British Cathedrals
J. MEIR	Northern Scenery
	Crow, Acorn & Oak Leaf Border
MINTON	Minton Miniatures
	British Views
E. & G. PHILLIPS	Park Scenery
POUNTNEY & ALLIES	River Thames
	Bristol Views
J. & W. RIDGWAY	Oxford & Cambridge colleges
	Rural Scenery
	Angus Seats
J. & R. RILEY	Large Scroll Border
	Union Border
J. & G. ROGERS	Rogers Views
W. SMITH	Select Views
	Baronial Halls
A. STEVENSON	Rose Border
R. STEVENSON & WILLIAMS	Acorn & Oak Leaf Border
	British Lakes
	Panoramic Scenery
	Lace Border
	Semi China Warranted
S. TAMS	Foliage Border
	Floral city
WALLACE	Rural Scenery
WEDGWOOD	Blue Rose Border
ENOCH WOOD	London Views
	Grapevine Border
	English Cities
	Rural Homes
MAKERS UNKNOWN	Antique Scenery
	British Views
	English Scenery
	Pineapple Border (attributed to J. Meir)
	British Scenery (attributed to Ridgway)
	Foliage Border
	British Palaces
	Diorama
	Tulip Border
	Morning Glory Border
	Flower Medallion Border

European and Oriental Views

Manufacturers	Pattern Series
ADAMS	Andalusia
	Cassino
	Palestine
	Spanish Convent
J. & M. P. BELL	Italian Lakes
T. & J. CAREY	Indian Temples
COPELAND & GARRETT	Byron Views
	Continental Scenery
CORK EDGE & MALKIN	Indian Scenery
	Marino
J. CARR & CO.	Dacca
DAVENPORT	Chinese in Gazebo
	Chinese Views
DON POTTERY	Named Italian Views
	Landscape
ELKIN KNIGHT	Canton Views
T. GODWIN	Indian Scenery
J. HALL	Oriental Scenery
R. HALL	Parisian Chateau
JOSEPH HEATH	Italian Villas
HERCULANEUM	French Scenery
	India
ELIJAH JONES	Denon's Egypt
	Picturesque Asiatic Beauties
JAMES KEELING	Views of Mesopotamia
MACHIN & POTTS	Continental Views
J. MEIR	Byron's Illustrations
	Italian Scenery
MINTON	Chinese Marine
	Dacca
J. RIDGWAY	Pomerania
J. & G. ROGERS	Athens
SPODE	Caramanian
TWIGG (NEW HILL)	Named Italian Views
ENOCH WOOD	Italian Scenery
	French Series
LEWIS WOOLF (FERRYBRIDGE)	Chinese Marine
MAKERS UNKNOWN	Oriental Scenery
	Royal Sketches
	Ottoman Empire (attributed to J. & W. Ridgway)
	Beauties of England and Wales
	Parrot Border (Pecking Parrots)
	Stafford Gallery
	Italian
	Italian Scenery (shell border)

American and Canadian Views

Examples for many of these views may be found in *Historical Staffordshire* by Jeffrey B. Snyder (1995).

Manufacturers	Pattern Series
ADAMS	Rose Medallion Border
G. L. ASHWORTH	American Marine (Lake)
E. F. BODLEY	American & Canadian
BOURNE NIXON & CO.	American & Canadian
J. & R. CLEWS	Picturesque Views
	American Views (States border)
	American Views (scroll medallion border)
R. COCHRANE	Quebec Views
DAVENPORT	Cities
T. GODWIN	American Views
W. GIMSON	The World (Canadian scenes)
JOSEPH HEATH	American Views
HENSHALL	Fruit and Flower Border
J. & J. JACKSON	Roses Border
C. MEIGH	American Cities and Scenery
MELLOR VENABLES	States Arms Border
PODMORE WALKER	British America
J. RIDGWAY	Log Cabin
W. RIDGWAY	Moss Border (American scenery)
	Catskill Moss Border
J. & W. RIDGWAY	Beauties of America
RIDGWAY, MORLEY & WEAR	Canadian Lakes
A. STEVENSON	American Views (floral scroll border)
	Portrait Medallion
RALPH STEVENSON & WILLIAMS	Acorn & Oak Leaf Border
	American Views (? vine border)
STUBBS	Eagle Border
	Rose Border
S. TAMS	Foliage Border (American views)
ENOCH WOOD	Boston Views
	Cockleshell Border
	Celtic China
	Shell Border
	Erie Canal
	Erie Canal Inscriptions
	Canadian Views
	Hudson River
	Four Medallion/floral border
MAKERS UNKNOWN	Cities (attributed to Clews)
	West Indian Views
	American Views (various borders)
	American Views (foliage and scroll border)

Sporting

Manufacturers	Pattern Series
E. CHALLINOR	Oriental Sports
J. & R. CLEWS	Hunting Views (Indian sporting)
COPELAND	Indian Sporting
DIMMOCK	Chevy Chase
GOODWIN & ELLIS	Peruvian Hunters
HERCULANEUM	Archery
	Field Sports
T. MAYER	Olympic Games
SPODE	Indian Sporting
ENOCH WOOD	Sporting

Animals and Birds

Manufacturers	Pattern Series
J. & R. CLEWS	Zoological Gardens
J. HALL	Quadrupeds
J. MEIGH	Zoological Sketches
J. MEIR	Childrens' Pets
ROBINSON WOOD & BROWNFIELD	Zoological
A. STEVENSON	Ornithological
WEDGWOOD	Blue Birdcage
MAKER UNKNOWN	Durham Ox

Literary, Artistic and Historical

Manufacturers	Pattern Series
ADAMS	Cupid
	Dr. Syntax (20th century reissue)
J. & R. CLEWS	Dr. Syntax
	Don Quixote (now possibly Davenport)
	Wilkie's Designs
COPELAND & GARRETT	Aesop's Fables
	Wellington
DAVENPORT	Scott's Illustrations
	Franklin's Morals
GOODWIN & HARRIS	Byron Gallery
J. & J. JACKSON	Holy Bible
JONES & SON	British History
C. J. MASON	Napoleon
T. MAYER	Illustrations of the Bible
MINTON	Fables (tile patterns)
E. & G. PHILLIPS	Polish Views
POUNTNEY & GOLDNEY	The Drama
W. RIDGWAY	Humphrey's Clock
BRAMELD (ROCKINGHAM)	Don Quixote
J. & G. ROGERS	The Drama
W. SMITH	Napoleon (Napoleon's Victories)
	Aesop's Fables
SPODE	Scriptural
ENOCH WOOD	Byron Gallery
MAKERS UNKNOWN	Franklin's Maxims
	Little Red Riding Hood
	Scottish Commemoratives
	Thomson's Seasons

American Historical and Others

Manufacturers	Pattern Series
ADAMS	Columbus Views
J. EDWARDS	Boston Mails
T. GODWIN	William Penn Treaty
T. MAYER	Arms of the States
J. MARSHALL	Canadian Sports
MELLOR VENABLES	Arms of the States
ANTHONY SHAW	Texian Campaign
TAMS ANDERSON & TAMS	Historical

Botanical

Manufacturers	Pattern Series
ELKIN & NEWBON	Botanical Beauties
E. & G. PHILLIPS	British Flowers
W. RIDGWAY	British Flowers
SPODE	Botanical
TURNER	Botanical Beauties
WEDGWOOD	Botanical
MAKER UNKNOWN	Strawberry Border
	Botanical Beauties (marked C.R.S.)

Classical

Manufacturers	Pattern Series
CLEMENTSON	Classical Antiques
ELKIN KNIGHT	Etruscan
FERRYBRIDGE	Greek
HERCULANEUM	Greek Key Border
T. J. & J. MAYER	Grecian Scroll
POUNTNEY & GOLDNEY	Antique Subjects
SPODE	Greek
MAKERS UNKNOWN	Greek Key Border
	Etruscan & Greek Vases

Romantic Views

Manufacturers	Pattern Series
BELLE VUE POTTERY	Chinese Marine
CHESWORTH & ROBINSON	Terni
DAVENPORT	Rhine
	Romantic Castles
DIMMOCK	Select Sketches
J. HALL	Antiquities
J. & J. JACKSON	Grecian Gardens
J. MEIR	Fairy Villas
MINTON	Genevese
MAKER UNKNOWN	No. 15

Miscellaneous

Manufacturers	Pattern Series
ADAMS	Seasons
COPELAND & GARRETT	Seasons
DAVENPORT	Chinese Pastimes
HICKS & MEIGH	Oriental Shells
J. RIDGWAY	Archipelago
RIDGWAY, MORLEY, WEAR	Pantheon
J. & G. ROGERS	Children's plates
R. STEVENSON	Semi-China Warranted (rural scenery)
	Pastoral
	Lace Border (views in England, America, and India)
STUBBS	Sea Shells
ENOCH WOOD	Shell Border (nautical views)
	Seaweed & Shells Border (Shipping series)
MAKERS UNKNOWN	Arctic Scenery (attributed to T. Godwin)
	British Marine
	Progress of the Loaf
	Children at Play
	Chinese Juvenile Sports
	Gipsy
	Seasons
	Pic-Nic